CONTENTS

PREFACE

This book is the result of many months of research and the generous assistance of experts in the field of errors. It is my hope that collectors will find it useful. Certain questionable items which may merit future listing were intentionally omitted from this edition pending more information about their true status. Also, errors of fact may exist in the listings or text. Anyone with information about inaccuaracies or omissions is encouraged to contact the publisher. Suggestions for revisions should be accompanied by documentable evidence or source for documentation. Your help will be appreciated.

ACKNOWLEDGMENT

Many individuals generously assisted in the preparation of this book by sharing their knowledge and opinions. Sincere thanks are extended to all of who have contributed. Special thanks are due Jacques C. Schiff, Jr. for his encouragment and resources in making this book a reality. Among those who have helped are:

Ken Beiner
Larry Bustillo
Bob Dumaine
Marvin Frey
Howard P. Gates, Jr.
Stan Goldfarb
Herman Herst, Jr.
Greg Hosler
John Hotchner

William S. Langs
Jack S. Molesworth
Jack Nalbandian
Daniel Pagter
James B. Peterson
D. James Samuelson
Robert A. Siegel
Martin Wilkinson

Note: Due to the volume of information received since publication of the first editon, it was necessary to extensively renumber listings.

INTRODUCTION

The scope of this work is U. S. postage stamps which contain certain major errors issued unintentionally and certain other stamps which may resemble errors, as in the case of certain imperforate stamps, which have reached the public domain by channels other than by which stamps would normally be sold or issued. Other categories of errors exist but are not presently within the scope of this catalogue.

Three categories of major errors are listed: stamps lacking perforations; multicolored stamps lacking one or more colors which would normally have been present; and stamps of two or more colors in which one of the design elements has been inverted during printing.

A normal stamp is defined as one which has been prepared according to specifications and put on sale to the public. An error stamp typically lacks an element (perforations or colors) due to a mistake in production and, therefore, would not intentionally be sold to the public.

To be considered an imperforate error, all perforations between two stamps must be missing. The presence of even one perforation or perforating pin impression disqualifies the stamp from being considered an imperforate error. The presence of incompletely impressed perforations, often referred to as "blind perfs", also disqualifies the stamp.

To be considered a color omitted error, all of the affected color(s) must be missing from the design. The presence of even a few dots of color disqualifies the stamp. The stamp must be able to pass scrutiny under 30 power or greater magnification. There are cases such as the Space Walk and First Man on the Moon stamps, where red in the flag or shoulder patch is described as omitted, however, dots of red lithographic color are present elsewhere on the stamp. In order to be classified as a true major error, all red color must be absent.

Albinos, stamps with all color(s) omitted, exist for certain issues but, for the present, are not included in this work. While it can be argued that they are color omitted errors, without the presence of any printing at all, it can be difficult to distinguish one from another.

Stamps with tagging omitted have not been separately listed. Tagging is applied by a separate printing plate and, although invisible to the naked eye, is considered by some be a "color" for purposes defining what should be present on a properly prepared stamp. However, for the purposes of this catalogue, stamps with tagging omitted have not been separately listed. In certain cases, the omission of tagging has been mentioned in conjunction with visible colors when it is known to have been omitted.

Traditionally, to be regarded as a "legitimate" error, a stamp must have found its way into public hands by inadvertent purchase across a post office counter. Several kinds of stamps, usually imperforates, have found their way into the philatelic domain by other means. While not errors in the traditional sense, they are often mistaken for errors by virtue of their appearance.

Because it is the purpose of this catalogue to be used as a reference, to aid in identification, and to foster knowledge, certain of these stamps are included herein. However, where they appear, they are identified by one of the references below.

PRF. *(Proof)* It is argued that many early imperforates are nothing more than proofs, prepared in issued colors on stamp paper, gummed or ungummed. Where the prevailing opinion is that the imperforate stamp was actually a stamp-like proof, the listing will be identified by **PRF.**

NRI. *(Not Regularly Issued)* Another class of imperforate stamps are those which were not regularly issued. While not put on sale to the public, imperforate stamps have been, on occasion, traded for services or rare items, such as the 1869 pictorial inverts, needed for the National Museum's collection. They are typically identical to their perforated counterparts, except for the lack of perforations. They were intentionally allowed to leave the hands of the government, are scarce and certainly collected. They are identified by **NRI.**

PW. *(Printers' Waste)* Another category of error stamp is known as "printer's waste." In printers' terminology "set-ups" or "make- readies" is paper used to get presses up and running smoothly. It is discarded as waste but occasionally finds its way into philatelic hands. On occasion, printers' waste, even after having been marked by government quality control inspectors for destruction, has found its way into philatelic hands by having been inadvertently included with regular shipments of stamps. On other occasions printers' waste has reached philatelic hands by having been purloined by employees at printing or waste paper facilities. Over the years the term "printers' waste," as used in philately, has taken on a pejorative connotation, referring to the manner in which suspect stamps reach the market, *i.e.* purloined stamps, not recognized nor esteemed by the philatelic community. In fact, many prefer not to include printers' waste in their collections. However, there are cases in which it is not clear how obviously imperfect stamps (either marked for destruction or generally faulty) reached public hands. Likewise, there are rare instances of perfectly legitimate looking stamps reaching the market, which might not otherwise be suspect except that it is known that they were misappropriated by an unscrupulous person in an inside position. For the purposes of this catalogue, the term printers' waste takes the traditional connotation, that of stamps having reached the market by suspect means. They are identified by **PW.**

Errors purchased and paid for over the post office counter are perfectly legal to own. However, it should be noted that purloined stamps remain the property of the United States Government and are not legal to own. Stamps which could not have been purchased at the post office, such as full uncut sheets of booklet panes, should be avoided, as they are government property.

FAKES

Fakes. Fakes of some errors exist. While many are crude, some are excellent and difficult to detect. Cautionary notes appear in the listings where appropriate. From a practical standpoint, the collector's best protection is in dealing with knowledgable, reputable dealers or requiring, at least for items of high value, that a certificate of authenticity by a recognized expertizing body be furnished.

Imperforate Singles. Generally they should be avoided. Certain 19th century issues are known as error singles. However, many 19th and 20th century stamps exist with huge margins which can be trimmed to resemble imperforates. Valid certificates of authenticity are necessary for imperforate singles.

Blind Perforations. Blind perforations can be ironed out and made invisible to the naked eye. This is especially true of stamps which have had the gum soaked off. The barest trace of even one perforation, even though it has not punched through, disqualifies the term "imperforate" from being applied. Pairs of stamps offered as imperforate should be carefully checked by a knowledgable authority.

Colors Omitted. Certain dyes used in printing are susceptible to removal or alteration by exposure to light, heat or chemicals. Many, such as the Copernicus yellow omitted, are easily created. Proper expertizing is recommended.

Inverts. Clever fakes exist created by cutting center designs and inverting them in relation to frames. The most clever do not cut entirely through the stamp's paper so that when viewed from the back, the gum and paper are intact.

Used Errors. Used errors should be checked extra carefully. Blind perfs can be ironed out and chemical treatments or other operations performed without having to worry about disturbing original gum, tagging or the pristineness of the stamp.

Expertizing. The publisher cannot give opinions as to the genuineness of errors. Not every error requires expertization. Often, a knowledgable dealer can verify an error or recommend expertizing if necessary. The two major expertizing organizations in the United States are the American Philatelic Society (APS), P. O. Box 8000, State College, PA 16803 (all errors) and the Philatelic Foundation, 270 Madison Avenue, New York, NY 10016 (PF does not render opinions on color omitted errors). Contact them directly for the forms necessary to submit a stamp for a certificate of authenticity.

HOW TO USE THE CATALOGUE

Listings are divided into sections according to type of error: imperforates, colors omitted and inverts. Listings are arranged as follows:

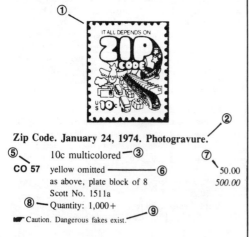

Zip Code. January 24, 1974. Photogravure.

10c multicolored — ③

CO 57 yellow omitted —————— ⑥   50.00
as above, plate block of 8   *500.00*
Scott No. 1511a
⑧ — Quantity: 1,000+
☛ Caution. Dangerous fakes exist.

1. Illustration. Each error is illustrated. Illustrations bordered in black are those of actual errors. Those lacking black borders are normal stamps used only to identify the issue. Photographs of actual errors were used wherever possible. Where an error photograph was not available, the illustration of a normal stamp is substituted. Illustrations of a normal stamps are also used in some cases where black and white reproduction does not adequately reveal the color omitted error.

2. Description. Each error is described by the subject of the stamp, date of issue, form (se-tenant, souvenir sheet, etc.), method of printing, perforation, watermark and type. *Watermark, perforation and type are given only when necessary to distinguish one stamp from another of similar design.*

3. Description. Denomination and color or colors are given. For imperforate errors only the color information necessary to identify the stamp is noted. For color omitted errors printed by a combination of presses, colors applied by each press are given along with the type of press. Individual colors applied by photogravure are not separately listed.

4. Designs. Where multiple stamp designs are contained se-tenant in an error, each individual design is identified.

5. Numbering. Errors are classified by category. Individual types within a category are identified by a prefix and number.

IM prefix identifies imperforate errors.

CO prefix identifies color(s) omitted errors.

IV prefix identifies center inverted errors.

A separate catalogue number is assigned to each error or variety. Under a specific listing, multiples such as plate blocks, Zip blocks, etc., are not separately numbered, being regarded as varieties in form of the basic type.

Gaps in the sequence of catalogue numbers may occur from time to time in anticipation of future listings.

In addition, each listing is cross referenced by a Scott number including suffix. Where the error is not listed in the Scott Catalogue, the Scott number for the normal stamp is given followed by the suffix "var", indicating a variety of the normal stamp.

6. Form. Following the catalogue number is a listing of the error in its basic or most commonly known form. Other forms of the error are listed beneath where known, for example, plate blocks and other multiples, used copies, covers, etc. The omission of a form, such as a plate block, does not necessarily mean that it does not exist, but only that it has not come to the attention of the publisher.

7. Price. Prices are based on the best information available including auctions, retail advertising and editors' judgment. Note well, that because the market determines values, prices for individual items may vary and at any given time, be more or less than those indicated here. That is especially true for newly discovered errors. Price will also vary with condition.

LRS. For very rare items, the Last Reported Sale is indicated by the initials LRS followed by the date in parentheses.

Italics. Prices in italics are the editors' estimates when no precise information is available. They should be regarded as tentative and subject to fluctuation. The actual market price for a specific item may be either higher or lower.

ERRORS

Inverts
Imperforates
Colors Omitted
On
United States Postage
Stamps

1988
Edition

Stephen R. Datz

GENERAL PHILATELIC CORPORATION
POST OFFICE BOX 402   LOVELAND, COLORADO 80539

ISBN: 0-88219-020-2 paperback
      0-88219-021-0 hardbound

Cover design: Marianne Garehime

Manufactured in the United States of America.

Published by General Philatelic Corporation
Post Office Box 402
Loveland, Colorado 80539
(303) 667-1133

—. A dash is used when no price listing is possible because of insufficient information, *e.g.* infrequently traded items or varieties such as plate blocks, etc. *The use of this symbol does not necessarily imply rarity.*

Prices for used modern errors on cover are for timely usage. Philatelically inspired covers are usually worth considerably less.

Pricing anomalies. Many errors exist in similar quantities but with different prices. *One cannot assume that there is a dependable ratio of quantity to price. The classic errors, e.g.* 1869 inverts or the inverted Jenny, sell for very high prices when compared with modern errors of similar quantity. Values of classic rarities have been established over time. Modern errors, as a group, are more plentiful. Generally, for modern errors, other factors being equal, the greater the eye appeal, the greater the price. Those which are not dramatic and not visually interesting tend to sell for less than more striking omissions of color or perforations. In many cases, plate or position error blocks do not command the premiums that their normal counterparts often do. Generally, position and multiple items are not as much in demand among error collectors as they are in the general collecting population. Also, there is some pressure to break multiples, even plate blocks, because they may be worth more on the market as individual pairs, etc.

Condition. Prices are for sound stamps, except where noted. Damaged or faulty copies may sell for substantial discounts. Hinging is to be expected on issues before 1940. Prices are for hinged copies in Fine to Very Fine (F-VF) condition. Better copies or NH copies may command substantial premiums. Prices for issues after 1940 are for Never Hinged (NH) copies in Fine to Very Fine (F-VF) condition.

8. Quantity. Quantities known or reliably reported to exist are listed. In many cases the the exact number existing is not ascertainable and therefore not given. Quantities given in italics are tentative and not considered firm, *e.g.* 100 pairs of a current stamp have been newly discovered and more may surface. Italics indicate the best information available at press time, albeit tentative.

Ranges are given, e.g. 50-100 pairs, where the general magnitude, but not the specific number, is acknowledged.

The term "reported" is used to indicate the quantity reported, by reliable sources, to exist. This number, especially on recent issues, is subject to change. In addition, several general terms are used to indicate quantity where exact information is not possible. The definitions are arbitrary but should be easier to remember than a series of letters or Roman numerals

Unique. Only one copy known.

Very Rare. Less than 10 copies believed to exist.

Rare. Less than 25 copies believed to exist.

Very Scarce. Less than 50 copies believed to exist.

Scarce. Less than 100 copies believed to exist.

Few Hundred. Generally 100-300 copies believed to exist.

Several Hundred. More than 300 copies believed to exist.

Few Thousand. Generally 1,000-3,000 copies believed to exist.

Several Thousand. More than 3,000 copies believed to exist.

N/a. Not available. No information available.

Quantities listed are subject to change as more information becomes available.

9. Notes. Information of interest to aid the reader. Cautionary notes, for fakes and the other potential problems, are given where appropriate and indicated by the sign ☞ .

DEFINITIONS

Blind Perforations. Incompletely or partially impressed perforations often barely indented into the paper and giving stamps the appearance of being imperforate. On some stamps, blind perforations have been ironed out resulting in the appearance of being imperforate. Because it is easier to iron out blind perforations in the absence of gum, ungummed imperforates should be examined closely under magnification.

Block. Four or more unseparated stamps arranged in a rectangle.

Booklet Pane. Small sheetlets of stamps bound by staples or glue between card stock covers.

Color Changlings. Colors on stamps which have been altered or eliminated by physical or chemical tampering. Certain stamp dyes are more susceptible to alteration, especially bleaching by sunlight, heat, or chemicals. Color changlings are of no philatelic value.

Engraving. Also known as intaglio. A method of printing in which the design is engraved (recessed) into a metal plate. Ink fills the recesses and, when printed, forms small ridges on the paper. Engraving can be identified by magnifying glass or often simply by running your finger over the surface of the stamp and feeling the ridges.

Flat Press. A printing press which utilizes flat plates and prints paper one sheet at a time.

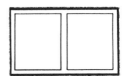

Imperforate. Lacking perforations. When used to describe a pair or multiple, imperforate means completely lacking perforations between stamps and on all sides.

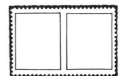

Imperforate Between. Lacking perforations between two or more stamps, but with perforations present on all outer sides. Pairs or multiples may be either horizontal or vertical.

Horizontal Pair, Imperforate Vertically. A pair of stamps, horizontally side by side, lacking vertical perforations between stamps and with vertical straight edges at either side. Perforations are present at the top or bottom of the pair.

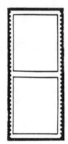

Vertical Pair, Imperforate Horizontally. A pair of stamps, one atop the other vertically, lacking horizontal perforations between stamps and with horizontal straight edges at either side. Perforations are present at left and right sides.

Imprint. A marginal inscription such as "American Bank Note Company" or "Bureau, Engraving & Printing." On modern issue "Use Zip Code", "Mail Early in the Day" and "Copyright USPS" often appear in margins.

Line Pair. On rotary press intaglio coil stamps, a line is created by ink, which fills the small space where two curved plates join, being printed much the same as ink from the recessed stamp design.

Lithography. Also known as planographic or surface printing. This process is based on the antipathy of water and oil. A photographic image is exposed to a photosensitive plate. The area exposed becomes water insoluble. The unexposed, water soluble area is washed away leaving an image which is receptive to ink. In some cases the inked image on the plate is transferred to a rubber-like blanket before being impressed on paper, hence the term offset printing.

Images are broken up into a series of dots in order to achieve tonal gradation. Color lithography involves the mingling of areas of dots from several plates in order to achieve the effect of color. Because each printing plate is only capable of laying down a single color, passes beneath several plates are necessary. These passes may occur in several press runs or in a single press run through a large press capable of mounting and running multiple plates. Stamp production typically involves from four to seven plates (colors). **Color errors are often produced when one or more plate impressions are omitted.** By examining any black and white or color printing, e.g. from a magazine or stamp, under a 10 power or stronger glass, you can observe the dot structure of lithography. You will see how the dots are used to yield tonal gradations and blend to make a variety of colors. In commercial printing four colors (plates) are typically used to achieve all colors; black, yellow, magenta and cyan. Stamp printing often employs additional plates, with a variety of specially mixed inkes, in order to achieve higher quality results.

Miscut. Cut abnormally so that portions of adjoining stamps appear together in the area normally occupied by a single design.

Pair. Two unseparated stamps.

Paste Up. The splicing or joining of paper, typically in web fed rotary printing, by glue or tape.

Photogravure. The gravure plate is also made by a photosensitive process, however, unlike lithography, the ink lies in small recesses and is very thinly applied. Tones can be achieved by varying the depth of the recesses and thickness of the ink. The image is broken up into a series of fine points which keep the paper from being pressed into the recesses. The dot structure in photogravure is usually much finer than that used in lithography. You can see the difference by comparing a magazine illustration with a photogravure stamp under a 10 power magnifying glass.

Plate Number. A serial number usually appearing in the margin of a sheet of stamps and infrequently on miscut coil or booklet stamps. Since about 1981, small plate numbers have appeared at the bottom of every nth stamp on many coil issues. Multicolored stamps usually, but not always, have a separate plate number for each color used in printing.

Rotary Press. A printing press on which the plates are curved in the form of a cylinder to facilitate the continuous printing of a web of paper.

Strip. Three or more unseparated stamps arranged side by side or end to end.

Tagging. A luminescent coating, applied during printing, used to facilitate the facing and handling or mail by automated machinery. Usually invisible to the naked eye, it can be observed under ultraviolet light. Tagging may cover all or part of the stamp.

Double Line Watermark

USPS

Single Line Watermark

Watermark. Letters impressed on paper during manufacture to discourage counterfeiting. Paper is thinner where the watermark has been impressed and, therefore, appears lighter when immersed in watermark detecting fluid.

TECHNICAL VOCABULARY
FACHAUSDRUCK VACABULAIRE TECHNIQUE VOCABULARIO TECNICO

ENGLISH	GERMAN	FRENCH	SPANISH
airmail	Flugpost	aerienne	aereo
bar	Balken	barre	barra
booklet	Heftchen	carnet	cuadernillo
bottom	Unten	bas	abajo
block	Block	bloc	bloque
block of 4	Viererblock	bloc de quatre	bloque de cuarto
cancellation	Abstempelung	obliteration	matasello
cancelled	entwertet	oblitere	usado, matasellado
coil	Markenrolle	rouleau de timbres	rollo de sellos
common	gewonlich	commun	comun
condition	Erhaltung	condition	estado (de conserv.)
color	Farbe	couleur	color
color shade	Farbton	nuance	variacion de color
cover	Briefumschlag	envelope	sobre
dash	Strich	trait	linea
definitive	Endgultig	definitif	definitivo
design	Zeichnung	dessin	diseno
engraved	graviert	grave	grabado
error	Fehler	erreur	error
expertised	gepruft	expertise	expertizado
fake	Falschung	faux	falsificacion
faulty	Mangelhaft	defautueux	defectuoso
genuine	echt	authentique	autentico
gum	Gummi	gomme	goma
hinge	Falz	charniere	fijasello
horizontal	liegand	couche	acostado
imperforate	ungezahnt	non dentele	sin dentar
inverted	kopfstehend	renverse	invertido
left	links	gauche	izquierda
lithographed	Steindruck	lithographie	litografia
margin	Rand	bord	carta
multiple	mehrfach	multiple	multiple
number	Nummer	numero	numero
numeral	Ziffer	chiffre	cifra
not regularly issued	nicht ausgege	ben non emis	no emitto
offset	Offsetdruck	decaler	impression calcada
pair	Paar	paire	pareja
perforated	gezahnt	dentele	dentado
photogravure	photogravure	heliogravure	huecograbado
postage due	Portomarke	timbre taxe	sello de tasa
postmark	Poststempel	cachet postale	matasello
price	Preis	prix	precio
proof	Probe	epreuve	prueba
rare	selten	rare	raro
reprint	Neudruck	reimpression	reimpresion
reverse	Ruckseite	verso	reverso
set	Satz	serie	serie
se-tenant	zusammendruck	se-tenant	combinacion
sheet	Bogen	feuille	hoja
souvenir sheet	Kleinbogen	bloc-feuillet	hoja bloca
special delivery	Eilmarke	expres	urgente
strip	Streifen	bande	tira
strip of 3	Dreierstreifen	bande de quatre	tira de tres
thick	dick	epais	grueso
thin	dunn	mince	delgado
top	Oben	haut	arriba
type	type	type	tipo
unused	ungebraucht	neuf	nuevo

TECHNICAL VOCABULARY
FACHAUSDRUCK VACABULAIRE TECHNIQUE VOCABULARIO TECNICO

ENGLISH	GERMAN	FRENCH	SPANISH
used	gebraucht	oblitere	usado, matasellado
variety	Abart	variete	variedad
vertical	hochstehend	vertical	vertical
watermark	Wasserzeichen	filigrane	filigrana
without	ohne	sans	sin
without gum	ohne Gummi	san gomme	fin goma

ABBREVIATIONS

hz	liegand	couche	acostado
imperf	ungezahnt	non dentele	sin dentar
litho	Steindruck	lithographie	litografia
No.	Nummer	numero	numero
NRI	nicht ausgege	ben non emis	no emitto
perf	gezahnt	dentele	dentado
PRF	Probe	epreuve	prueba
vrt	hochstehend	vertical	vertical

COLORS

bistre	gelbraun	bistre	sepia
black	schwarz	noir	negro
blue	blau	bleu	azul
bright	lebhaft	vif	vivo
brown	braun	brun	castano
buff	samisch	chamois	anteado
carmine	karmin	carmin	carmin
chocolate	schokoladen	chocolat	chocolate
claret	weinrot	lie de vin	rojo vinoso
dark	dunkel	fonce	oscuro
deep	tief	fonce	subido
dull	trub	terne	color apagado
flesh	fleischfarben	chair	carne
gray	grau	gris	gris
green	grun	vert	verde
indigo	indigo	indigo	azul indigo
lake	lackfarbe	lie de vin	laca
light	hell	clair	claro
lilac	lila	lilas	lila
magenta	magentarot	magenta	magenta
multicolored	mehrfarbig	polychrome	multicolores
ochre	ocker	ocre	ocre
olive	oliv	olive	aceintuna
orange	orange	orange	naranja
pale	blass	pale	palido
pink	rosa	rose	rosa
Prussian blue	preussisch blau	bleu de Presse	azul de Prusia
purple	purpur	pourpre	purpura
red	rot	rouge	rojo
rose	rosa	rose	rosa
scarlet	scharlach	ecarlate	escarlata
ultramarine	ultramarin	outremer	ultramar
vermilion	zinnober	vermillon	bermellon
violet	violett	violet	violeta
white	weiss	blanc	blanco
yellow	gelb	juane	amarillo

IMPERFORATE ERRORS

SERIES OF 1857/61

Benjamin Franklin. July 1857. Engraved, printed by Toppan, Carpenter & Co.

1c blue, type IIIa

IM 1 used hz pair, imperf between   —
Scott No. 22b
Quantity: very rare

Benjamin Franklin. 1857. Engraved, printed by Toppan, Carpenter & Co.

1c blue, type V

IM 2 used vrt strip of 5, imperf
hz LRS (83)   2,300.00
Scott No. 24c
Quantity: unique

1c FRANKLIN DESIGNS OF THE 1857/61 SERIES

Type IIIa is as illustrated but with either the top or bottom frame line cut away, but not both. The side ornaments are complete.
Type V is similar to Type III but has the side ornaments partially cut away.

George Washington. 1857. Engraved, printed by Toppan, Carpenter & Co.

3c rose, type I

IM 3 used hz pair, imperf vrt   —
Scott No. 25a
Quantity: very rare

IM 4 used vrt pair, imperf hz   —
Scott No. 25b
Quantity: very rare

IM 3 and IM 4 were printed from the same plates as the imperforate 1851 series. Regularly issued imperforate stamps of the 1851 series should not be confused with errors of the 1857 series. Also, proofs of the 1851 series in issued colors were printed on bond paper very similar in appearance to stamp paper. The two are so similar that it very difficult, especially for the unpracticed eye, to distinguish one from another.

3c WASHINGTON DESIGNS OF THE 1857/61 SERIES

Type I has a frame line intact all around.
Type II has the frame line removed at the top and bottom. The side frame lines are continuous from stamp to stamp.

George Washington. 1857. Engraved, printed by Toppan, Carpenter & Co.

3c dull red, type II

IM 5   hz pair, imperf vrt   —
as above, used   —
Scott No. 26b
Quantity: very rare

IM 6   used vrt pair, imperf hz   —
Scott No. 26c
Quantity: very rare

IM 7   used hz pair, imperf between   —
Scott No. 26d
Quantity: very rare

George Washington. 1857. Engraved, printed by Toppan, Carpenter & Co.

12c black

IM 8   used hz pair, imperf between
LRS   2,475.00
Scott No. 36c
Quantity: very rare

George Washington. 1860. Engraved, printed by Toppan, Carpenter & Co.

24c gray or gray lilac

IM 9   imperf pair   20,000.00
single, imperf   1,000.00
Scott No. 37c
Quantity: 2 pairs reported,
singles very rare

In his book *Postage Stamps of the United States*, John Luff claims to "have seen 2 copies used on original envelopes." He thinks perhaps a sheet got out. Lester Brookman claims these (24c-30c-90c) were trial printings submitted by Toppan, Carpenter & Co. to the Postmaster General and therefore not regularly issued.

Benjamin Franklin. 1860. Engraved, printed by Toppan, Carpenter & Co.

30c orange

IM 10   imperf pair   6,900.00
single, imperf   2,000.00
Scott No. 38a
Quantity: 3 pairs reported;
singles very rare

Refer to note following IM 9. John Luff states that a used single, printed in the brown orange shade peculiar to imperfs, exists on cover to France.

George Washington. August 1860. Engraved, printed by Toppan, Carpenter & Co.

90c blue

IM 11   imperf pair   30,000.00
single, imperf   3,500.00
Scott No. 39a
Quantity: 1 pair reported;
singles very rare

Lester Brookman states that a used single, with "good margins", appeared in the Pelander sale of February 1943. It is mentioned here for the record.

☛ 19th Century stamps often occur with large margins which can be trimmed to resemble imperforates. Single stamps, even margin copies, should be regarded with suspicion. Imperforate singles without certificates of authenticity should be avoided.

SERIES OF 1857/1860

SPECIAL PRINTING OF 1875

Engraved. Printed by the Continental Bank Note Company on bright, white paper, without gum. Imperforates are varieties of the perforated stamps issued for the Centennial Exposition of 1876.

IM 12   1c Franklin, bright blue

IM 13   3c Washington, scarlet

IM 14   5c Jefferson, orange brown

IM 15   10c Washington, blue green

IM 16   12c Washington, greenish black

IM 17   24c Washington, blackish violet

IM 18   30c Franklin, yellow orange

IM 19   90c Washington, deep blue
set of 8 pairs, imperf —
set of 8 margin singles, imperf
LRS (85)   41,250.00
Scott Nos. 40-47 var
respectively
Quantity: singles very rare; 1
set of pairs reported

SERIES OF 1861/1862

Printed by the National Bank Note Company.

Benjamin Franklin. August 17, 1861. Engraved

1c blue

IM 20   used vrt pair, imperf hz   —
Scott No. 63d
Quantity: very rare

George Washington. August 17, 1861. Engraved.

3c rose red or various
shades

IM 21   imperf pair   **PRF**   750.00
block of 4, imperf   1,750.00
block of 8, imprint & plate No. 11   —
Scott No. 65c
Quantity: scarce

IM 22   vrt pair, imperf hz   —
Scott No. 65d
Quantity: rare

3c lake

IM 23   imperf pair   2,250.00
bottom imprint & plate No. 52
block of 8, imperf   *15,000.00*
Scott No. 66a
Quantity: scarce, imprint block
of 8 unique

Trial color proofs were printed from Plate No. 34. The unique bottom
block of 8 is from Plate No. 52.

George Washington. August 20, 1861. Engraved.

10c green

IM 24   used vrt pair, imperf hz
Scott No. 68b
Quantity: very rare, possibley
unique

George Washington. February 20, 1863. Engraved.

24c dark gray

IM 29   vrt pair, imperf **NRI**   *1,500.00*
used single, imperf   —
Scott No. 78 var
Quantity: 1-3 pairs known

STAMPS WITH GRILLS

Grills, waffle-like in appearance, were impressed on stamps to break the paper fibers and allow more ink to be absorbed, preventing washing and reuse. Several types of grills exist.

A grill: points up covering
entire stamp.
C grill: points up, grill
measures about 13x16 mm.
F grill: points down, grill
measures about 9x13 mm.

George Washington. 1867. Engraved.

3c rose, A grill

IM 30   imperf pair   **NRI**   —
bottom imprint block of 8,
imperf LRS (75)   *8,000.00*
Scott No. 79a
Quantity: very rare

3c rose, C grill

IM 31   imperf pair   **NRI**   1,650.00
margin single with selvedge,
imperf   *1,000.00*
Scott No. 83a
Quantity: n/a

3c red or rose red, F grill

IM 32   imperf pair   *650.00*
Scott No. 94b
Quantity: very rare

IM 33   vrt pair, imperf hz   —
Scott No. 94c
Quantity: very rare

SERIES OF 1869
SPECIAL PRINTING OF 1875

Columbus. 1875. Engraved, printed by the National Bank Note Co.

15c brown & blue

IM 35   single, imperf hz   1,600.00
Scott No. 129a
Quantity: *very rare*

SERIES OF 1870/1871

Printed by the National Bank Note Company.

George Washington. April 1870. Engraved.

3c green, with grill

IM 36	imperf pair	1,250.00
	Scott No. 136b	
	Quantity: *very scarce*	

3c green, without grill

IM 37	imperf pair	—
	block of ten with bottom imprint & plate No. 11, imperf	5,500.00
	Scott No. 147c	
	Quantity: *rare*	

SERIES OF 1873

Printed by the Continental Bank Note Company. Stamps of this series contain secret marks as illustrated.

Benjamin Franklin. 1873. Engraved. With secret mark.

1c ultramarine

IM 38	imperf pair	—
	used imperf pair LRS (78)	500.00
	Scott. 156f	
	Quantity: approx 15 pairs	

SECRET MARKS OF THE BANKNOTE SERIES

1c secret mark is a small curved mark in the pearl at the left of the numeral "1".

3c secret mark is a strengthening of the shaded ribbon beneath the letters "RE".

10c secret mark is a small semicircle in the scroll on the right side of the design.

Andrew Jackson. 1873. Engraved. With secret mark.

2c brown

IM 39	imperf pair	—
	Scott No. 157 var	
	Quantity: *very rare*	

Andrew Jackson. June 21, 1875. Engraved.

2c vermilion

IM 40	imperf pair **PRF**	600.00
	block of 4, imperf	1,400.00
	Scott No. 178a	
	Quantity: scarce	

George Washington. 1873. Engraved. With secret mark.

    3c green

IM 41   imperf pair   **PRF**   —
          Scott No. 158g

IM 42   used hz pair, imperf vrt   —
          Scott No.: 158h

IM 43   used hz pair, imperf between   —
          Scott No. 158i
          Quantity: *rare*

    3c green, with grill

IM 44   imperf pair   **PRF**   —
          Scott No. 158f
          Quantity: n/a

Grills, waffle-like in appearance, were impressed on stamps to break the paper fibers and allow more ink to be absorbed, preventing washing and reuse. Several types of grills exist.

Thomas Jefferson. 1873. Engraved. With secret mark.

    10c brown

IM 45   hz pair, imperf between   —
          used imperf pair   *2,750.00*
          Scott No. 161d
          Quantity: very rare

SERIES OF 1879

Issues of the American Bank Note Company.

George Washington. 1879. Engraved.

    3c green

IM 46   imperf pair   **PRF**   —
          Scott No. 184a
          Quantity: *rare*

Thomas Jefferson. 1879. Engraved. With secret mark.

    10c brown

IM 47   used vrt pair, imperf between   —
          Scott No. 188c
          Quantity: *rare*

Commodore O. H. Perry. 1879. Engraved.

    90c carmine

IM 48   imperf pair   **PRF**   *2,500.00*
          block of four, imperf   *5,500.00*
          Scott No. 191b
          Quantity: *rare*

George Washington. 1883. Engraved.

2c red brown

IM 49   imperf pair   **NRI**   —
Scott No. 210b
Quantity: *rare*

SPECIAL PRINTING OF 1883

George Washington. 1883. Engraved. Soft porous paper.

2c pale red brown

IM 50   hz pair, imperf between   2,000.00
part sheet of 66 with right six
pairs imperf between - affixed
to cardboard LRS (5/87)   17,600.00
Scott No. 211Bc
Quantity: 10-20 pairs

Andrew Jackson. October 1, 1883. Engraved.

4c blue green

IM 51   imperf pair   **PRF or NRI**   —
Scott No. 211a
Quantity: *scarce*

Benjamin Franklin. June 11, 1887. Engraved.

1c ultramarine

IM 52   imperf pair   —
used imperf pair   —
Scott No. 212a
Quantity: *rare*

A horizontal strip of 3 and a horizontal strip on cover postmarked Hoboken, New Jersey, have been reported.

George Washington. September 10, 1887. Engraved.

2c green

IM 54   imperf pair   —
used imperf pair   *360.00*
imperf pair on cover   —
Scott No. 213a
Quantity: one pair unused; one
pair and one used strip of 3
reported.

James A. Garfield. February 10, 1888. Engraved.

5c indigo

IM 55   imperf pair   **PRF**   1,100.00
Scott No. 216b
Quantity: rare

Alexander Hamilton. January 3, 1888. Engraved.

30c orange brown

IM 56   imperf pair   **PRF**   *1,300.00*
Scott No. 217a
Quantity: rare

Often contains faults.

Commodore O. H. Perry. February 28, 1888. Engraved.

90c purple

IM 57   imperf pair   **PRF**   —
Scott No. 218a
Quantity: rare

ISSUES OF THE AMERICAN BANK NOTE COMPANY SMALL FORMAT 1890/93

In order to acquire rare stamps for the official collection at the National Museum, imperforate stamps, identical to their perforated counterparts, were exchanged for items needed such as the 1869 inverts. A total of 56 imperforate sets, mostly in pairs and blocks of four, were released. Imperforate postage due stamps, 1891 series, were simultaneously released. Refer to the postage due section for those issues.

In addition, proofs of the 2, 4, and 5 cents denominations in various shades similar to the issued colors, on gummed stamp paper, exist. The two cent denomination reportedly exists in five shades; the four cent in 11 shades; and the five cent in 13 shades. They should not be confused with the imperforate stamps listed below.

Benjamin Franklin. February 22, 1890. Engraved.

1c dull blue

IM 58   imperf pair   **NRI**   225.00
block of 4, imperf   475.00
Scott No. 219c
Quantity: 56

George Washington. February 22, 1890. Engraved.

2c lake

IM 59   imperf pair   **NRI**   100.00
block of 4, imperf   225.00
Scott No. 219De
Quantity: 56

2c carmine, May 12, 1890

IM 60   imperf pair   **NRI**   100.00
block of 4, imperf   225.00
block of 12 with plate No. 180
& inscription American Bank
Note Co., imperf   *1,000.00*
Scott No. 220d
Quantity: 56

Andrew Jackson. February 22, 1890. Engraved.

3c purple

IM 61   imperf pair   **NRI**   225.00
block of 4, imperf   525.00
Scott No. 221a
Quantity: 56

Abraham Lincoln. June 2, 1890. Engraved.

4c dark brown

IM 62	imperf pair **NRI**	250.00
	block of 4, imperf	525.00
	Scott No. 222a	
	Quantity: 56	

Ulysses S. Grant. June 2, 1890. Engraved.

5c chocolate brown

IM 63	imperf pair **NRI**	275.00
	block of 4, imperf	575.00
	block of 12 with top imprint	
	imperf	—
	Scott No. 223b	
	Quantity: 56	

James A. Garfield. February 22, 1890. Engraved.

6c brown red

IM 64	imperf pair **NRI**	300.00
	block of 4, imperf	625.00
	Scott No. 224a	
	Quantity: 56	

William T. Sherman. March 21, 1893. Engraved.

8c lilac

IM 65	imperf pair **NRI**	1,250.00
	block of 4, imperf	—
	Scott No. 225a	
	Quantity:	

Daniel Webster. February 22, 1890. Engraved.

10c green

IM 66	imperf pair **NRI**	400.00
	block of 4, imperf	850.00
	Scott No. 226a	
	Quantity: 56	

Henry Clay. February 22, 1890. Engraved.

15c indigo

IM 67	imperf pair **NRI**	775.00
	block of 4, imperf	1,700.00
	Scott No. 227a	
	Quantity: 56	

Thomas Jefferson. February 22, 1890. Engraved.

30c black

IM 68	imperf pair	**NRI**	1,375.00
	block of 4, imperf		3,000.00
	Scott No. 228a		
	Quantity: 56		

Commodore O. H. Perry. February 22, 1890. Engraved.

90c orange

IM 69	imperf pair	**NRI**	2,750.00
	block of 4, imperf		5,750.00
	Scott No. 229a		
	Quantity: 56		

COLUMBIAN SERIES OF 1893

The B. K. Miller Collection at the New York Public Library Collection contains a complete set of horizontal pairs, 1c-$5. They were originally the property of John Wanamaker, Postmaster General 1889-93.

Columbus Landing. January 2, 1893. Engraved.

2c purple maroon

IM 70	imperf pair, ungummed	**PW**	1,250.00
	as above, block of 4		—
	Scott No. 231b		
	Quantity: *50-100*		

These stamps are from a crumpled sheet, thought to be printer's waste. All known copies are ungummed and defective.

SERIES OF 1894

Similar to the Series of 1890 except triangles added to the upper corners. Printed on unwatermarked paper.

George Washington. October 5, 1894. Engraved.

2c pink, Type I

IM 71	vrt pair, imperf hz	2,250.00
	Scott No. 248a	
	Quantity: *rare*	

2c carmine, Type I

IM 72	vrt pair, imperf hz	—
	Scott No. 250a	
	Quantity: *rare*	

IM 73	hz pair, imperf between	—
	Scott No. 250b	
	Quantity: *rare*	

 Type I   Type II   Type III

2c WASHINGTON DESIGNS OF 1894

Type I has horizontal lines of the same thickness inside and outside the triangle.
Type II has horizontal lines which cross the triangle but are thinner inside it than outside it.
Type III has thin lines inside the triangle but these do not cross the double frame line of the triangle.

2c carmine, type III

IM 74   hz pair, imperf vrt   —
Scott No. 252a
Quantity: *rare*

IM 75   hz pair, imperf between   —
Scott No. 252b
Quantity: *rare*

Andrew Jackson. September 24, 1894. Engraved.

3c purple

IM 76   imperf pair, ungummed **NRI**   250.00
imperf block of 4, ungummed   550.00
plate block of 6 with imprint
and number, imperf, ungummed
Scott No. 253a
Quantity: 400

IM 76 was issued without gum. Those with gum had it added later.

Abraham Lincoln. September 11, 1894. Engraved.

4c dark brown

IM 77   imperf pair, ungummed **NRI**   *300.00*
imperf block of 4, ungummed   —
plate block of 6 with imprint
and number, imperf, ungummed
Scott No. 254a
Quantity: 400

IM 77 was issued without gum. Those with gum had it added later.

Ulysses S. Grant. September 28, 1894. Engraved.

5c chocolate brown

IM 78   imperf pair, ungummed **NRI**   350.00
imperf block of 4, ungummed   700.00
plate block of 6 with imprint
and plate number, imperf,
ungummed   —
Scott No. 255b
Quantity: 300-400

IM 78 was issued without gum. Those with gum had it added later.

IM 79   vrt pair, imperf hz, with gum   1,100.00
Scott No. 255c
Quantity: uncertain, but
reportedly less than one sheet of
100 was found.

James A. Garfield. July 18, 1894. Engraved.

6c dull brown

IM 80   vrt pair, imperf hz   *1,000.00*
block of 4, imperf hz   —
Scott No. 256a
Quantity: 100

Daniel Webster. September 17, 1894. Engraved.

10c dark green

IM 81 imperf pair, ungummed **NRI** —
imperf block of 4, ungummed —
Scott No. 258a
Quantity: 400

IM 81 was issued without gum. Those with gum had it added later.

Lester Brookman mentions that the 50c denomination was reported as a single on cover. Also, Brookman describes a bottom margin pair with perforations missing between the bottoms of the stamps and the selvedge. He mentions also that the $1 denomination, type I (Scott No. 261) exists imperforate but does not mention its form, i.e., horizontal, vertical or imperforate between.

SERIES OF 1895

Similar to the Series of 1894 except with watermark USPS horizontally or vertically.

Like the Series of 1890, quantities of imperforate stamps of this series reached public hands, this time via Gilbert Jones, owner of the New York Times, who accepted them in exchange for services rendered to the Bureau of Engraving and Printing. They are gummed and identical to regular stamps of this series except for the lack of perforations. It is reported that the 1-2-3-4 and 8c denominations exist used philatelically on cover.

Benjamin Franklin. January 17, 1898. Engraved. Double line watermark.

1c dull blue

IM 82 imperf pair **NRI** 250.00
block of 4, imperf 500.00
block of 6 with plate number
and imprint, imperf 1,850.00
used imperf pair, on cover —
Scott No. 264c
Quantity: 900

IM 83 hz pair, imperf vrt —
plate strip of 3, imperf vrt —
Scott No. 264b
Quantity: 1-5

George Washington. 1895. Engraved. Double line watermark.

2c carmine, Type III

IM 84 imperf pair **NRI** 250.00
block of 4, imperf 500.00
vrt strip of 3 with imprint and
plate number, imperf —
Scott No. 267a
Quantity: 500

Andrew Jackson. October 31, 1895. Engraved. Double line watermark.

3c dark purple violet

IM 85 imperf pair **NRI** 300.00
block of 4, imperf 600.00
used imperf pair, on cover —
Scott No. 268a
Quantity: 300

Abraham Lincoln. June 5, 1895. Engraved. Double line watermark.

4c black brown

IM 86 imperf pair **NRI** 350.00
block of 4, imperf 800.00
used imperf pair, on cover —
Scott No. 269a
Quantity: 300

Ulysses S. Grant. June 11, 1895. Engraved. Double line watermark.

5c deep reddish brown

IM 87	imperf pair **NRI**	350.00
	block of 4, imperf	800.00
	Scott No. 270b	
	Quantity: 300	

Daniel Webster. June 7, 1895. Engraved. Double line watermark.

10c pale dull green

IM 90	imperf pair **NRI**	500.00
	block of 4, imperf	1,050.00
	Scott No. 273a	
	Quantity: 400	

James A. Garfield. August 31, 1895. Engraved. Double line watermark.

6c claret brown

IM 88	imperf pair **NRI**	350.00
	block of 4, imperf	750.00
	top margin block of 6 with plate	
	No. 373	*4,000.00*
	Scott No. 271b	
	Quantity: 300	

Henry Clay. September 10, 1895. Engraved. Double line watermark.

15c deep indigo

IM 91	imperf pair **NRI**	1,250.00
	block of 4, imperf	—
	Scott No. 274a	
	Quantity: 100	

William T. Sherman. July 22, 1895. Engraved. Double line watermark.

8c deep claret brown

IM 89	imperf pair **NRI**	550.00
	block of 4, imperf	1,250.00
	used imperf pair, on cover	—
	Scott No. 272b	
	Quantity: 300	

Thomas Jefferson. November 9, 1895. Engraved. Double line watermark.

50c orange

IM 92	imperf pair **NRI**	1,400.00
	block of 4, imperf	2,950.00
	Scott No. 275b	
	Quantity: 100	

Commodore O. H. Perry. August 12, 1895. Engraved. Double line watermark.

$1 black, type I

IM 93   imperf pair   **NRI**   2,000.00
            block of 4, imperf   4,250.00
            Scott No. 276b
            Quantity: 100

James Madison. August 13, 1895. Engraved. Double line watermark.

$2 blue

IM 94   imperf pair   **NRI**   3,500.00
            block of 4, imperf   7,500.00
            Scott No. 277b
            Quantity: 100

John Marshall. August 16, 1895. Engraved. Double line watermark.

$5 dark green

IM 95   imperf pair   **NRI**   6,000.00
            block of 4, imperf   13,500.00
            Scott No. 278a
            Quantity: 100

$1 PERRY DESIGNS OF 1894

Type I contains circles around the "$1" which are broken at the the point of contact with the curved framed line below "One Dollar".
Type II contains complete circles.

TRANS-MISSISSIPPI SERIES OF 1898

Troops Guarding Train. June 1893. Engraved.

8c violet brown

IM 96   vrt pair, imperf hz   12,500.00
            vrt strip of 4, imperf hz LRS
            (85)   20,900.00
            block of 6, top or bottom plate
            number, imperf hz   —
            Scott No. 289a
            Quantity: 25 pairs

SERIES OF 1902/03

George Washington. November 12, 1903. Engraved.

2c carmine

IM 97 vrt pair, imperf hz   *1,250.00*
Scott No. 319d
Quantity: rare

IM 98 vrt pair, imperf between   —
Scott No. 319e
Quantity: rare

Do not confuse the 2c stamps listed here with similar stamps of 1906 which were regularly issued imperforate.

LOUISIANA PURCHASE EXPOSITION

Thomas Jefferson. April 30, 1904. Engraved.

2c carmine

IM 99 vrt pair, imperf hz   5,000.00
Scott No. 324a
Quantity: 25 pairs

WASHINGTON-FRANKLIN SERIES OF 1912/18

George Washington. February 12, 1912. Engraved. Single line watermark. Perf 12.

1c green

IM 100 vrt pair, imperf hz   *750.00*
vrt strip of three, imperf hz   —
Scott No. 405a
Quantity: *rare*

Do not confuse IM 100 with the stamp of identical design (Scott No. 408) which was regularly issued imperforate.

George Washington. 1910. Engraved. Single line watermark. Perf 10.

1c green

IM 101 vrt pair, imperf hz   400.00
used vrt pair, imperf hz   —
Scott No. 424c
Quantity: n/a

IM 102 booklet pane of 6, ungummed,
imperf   *700.00*
Scott No. 424d var
Quantity: 100 reported

George Washington. 1917. Engraved. No watermark. Perf 11.

1c green

IM 103 vrt pair, imperf hz   200.00
           block of 4, imperf hz   400.00
           Scott No. 498a
           Quantity: 1 sheet of 100 reported

IM 104 hz pair, imperf between   75.00
           Scott No. 498b
           Quantity: n/a

IM 105 vrt pair, imperf between   —
           Scott No. 498c
           Quantity: *scarce*

George Washington. 1917. Engraved. No watermark. Perf 11.

2c rose, type I

IM 106 vrt pair, imperf hz   175.00
           Scott No. 499a
           Quantity: n/a

IM 107 hz pair, imperf vrt   125.00
           used hz pair, imperf vrt   —
           Scott No. 499b
           Quantity: 100 pairs reported

IM 108 vrt pair, imperf between   450.00
           used vrt pair, imperf between   —
           Scott No. 499c
           Quantity: *very scarce*

☞ Caution. These stamps are known with blind perfs which can be ironed out and eliminated to the naked eye, resulting in dangerous fakes. Copies lacking gum should be regarded with special caution.

TYPES OF THE WASHINGTON-FRANKLIN SERIES

Type I

2c **Type I** has one line of shading in the ribbon on each side per illustration. Toga button has faint outline and top line is very faint.

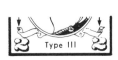

2c Type III has two lines of shading in ribbons and heavy lines in toga button and toga top line. Occurs on rotary press printings only.

2c Type V has strong top line of toga and toga button has five vertical engraved lines. The line of color in the left "2" is very thin and often broken. Occurs on offset printing only.

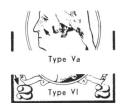

2c Type Va is similar to Type V except in the shading dots on the nose. The third row from the bottom has four dots instead of six. Occurs on offset printings only.

2c Type VI is similar to Type V except that the line of color in the left "2" is very heavy. Occurs on offset printings only.

3c WASHINGTON DESIGNS

3c Type I has weak the top line of toga and shading lines joining toga. The fifth line from the left is partly cut away at top and the line between the lips is thin. Occurs on flat and rotary press printings.

George Washington. 1917. Engraved. No watermark. Perf. 11.

3c violet, type I

IM 109   vrt pair, imperf hz   300.00
Scott No. 501c
Quantity: *very scarce*

3c dark violet, type II

IM 110   vrt pair, imperf hz   *250.00*
used vrt pair, imperf hz   —
Scott No. 502c
Quantity: 40-50 pairs reported

George Washington. 1917. Engraved. No watermark. Perf 11.

5c blue

IM 111   hz pair, imperf between   1,600.00
hz pair, imperf between, plate
No. 8902 in top margin   —
Scott No. 504a
Quantity: *very rare*

Benjamin Franklin. 1917. Engraved. No watermark. Perf 11.

8c olive bistre

IM 112   vrt pair, imperf between   —
used vrt pair, imperf between   —
Scott No. 508b
Quantity: 1 pair unused, 2 pair
used reported

Benjamin Franklin. 1917. Engraved. No watermark. Perf 11.

20c light ultramarine

IM 113 vrt pair, imperf between 300.00
Scott No. 515b
Quantity: rare

☛ Caution. These stamps are often encountered with blind perfs which can be ironed out and eliminated to the naked eye, resulting in dangerous fakes. Copies lacking gum should be regarded with special caution. The discovery sheets of this error contained mostly pairs with blind perforations and yielded only about 5 truly imperf pairs per sheet. As noted, the blind pairs are comparatively plentiful and can be deceptive.

Benjamin Franklin. 1917. Engraved. No watermark. Perf 11.

50c red violet

IM 114 vrt pair, imperf between _1,800.00_
used vrt pair, imperf between —
Scott No. 517b
Quantity: very rare

George Washington. 1918. Offset lithography. No watermark. Perf 11.

1c gray green

IM 115 hz pair, imperf between 65.00
Scott No. 525c
Quantity: n/a

IM 115 often has a straight edge on the right.

George Washington. 1919. Engraved. Rotary Press. No watermark. Design measures 19.5 to 20mm by 22 to 22.5mm. Perf 11x10.

1c green

IM 116 vrt pair, imperf hz 45.00
used vrt pair, imperf hz —
block of 4, imperf hz 90.00
block of 6, top plate number,
imperf hz 525.00
Scott No. 538a
Quantity: 1,000+

George Washington. 1919. Offset lithography. No watermark. Perf 12 1/2.

1c gray green

IM 117 hz pair, imperf vrt 400.00
block of 4, imperf vrt 800.00
Scott No. 536a
Quantity: n/a

George Washington. 1919. Engraved. Rotary press. No watermark. Design measures 19.5 to 20mm by 22 to 22.25mm. Perf 11x10.

2c carmine rose, type III

IM 118	vrt pair, imperf hz	50.00
	used vrt pair, imperf hz	*50.00*
	block of 4, imperf hz	100.00
	Scott No. 540a	
	Quantity: 1,000+	

IM 119	hz pair, imperf vrt	400.00
	Scott No. 540b	
	Quantity: 25 pairs reported	

George Washington. 1920. Offset lithography. No watermark. Perf 11.

2c carmine, type V

IM 120	vrt pair, imperf hz	*700.00*
	Scott No. 527b	
	Quantity: *2-3 pairs reported*	

IM 121	used hz pair, imperf vrt	—
	Scott No. 527c	
	Quantity: n/a	

Do not confuse IM 120 and IM 121 with the regularly issued imperforate (Scott No. 533) of the same design.

George Washington. 1920. Offset lithography. No watermark. Perf 11.

2c carmine, type Va

IM 122	vrt pair, imperf between	*2,400.00*
	Scott No. 528g	
	Quantity: n/a	

Do not confuse IM 122 with the regularly issued imperforate (Scott No. 534) of the same design.

George Washington. 1920. Offset lithography. No watermark. Perf 11.

2c carmine, type VI

IM 123	vrt pair, imperf hz	—
	Scott No. 528Af	
	Quantity: very rare	

IM 124	vrt pair, imperf between	—
	Scott No. 528Ah	
	Quantity: very rare	

Do not confuse IM 124 with the regularly issued imperforate (Scott No. 534A) of the same design.

George Washington. 1921. Engraved. Rotary press. No watermark. Design measures 19.5 by 22 mm. Perf 10.

1c green

IM 125	hz pair, imperf between	*500.00*
	Scott No. 543a	
	Quantity: *rare*	

SERIES OF 1922/26

Stamps of 1922/26 series were printed by flat plate press and normally perforated 11. Designs measure 18.5 to 19mm by 22mm.

Nathan Hale. April 4, 1925. Engraved.

1/2c dark brown

IM 127 block of 4, imperf,
ungummed **NRI**   —
Scott No. 551 var
Quantity: unique

Benjamin Franklin. January 17, 1923. Engraved.

1c green

IM 128 block of 4, imperf,
ungummed **NRI**   —
Scott No. 552 var
Quantity: unique

Warren G. Harding. March 19, 1925. Engraved.

1 1/2c brown

IM 129 block of 4, imperf,
ungummed **NRI**   —
Scott No. 553 var
Quantity: unique

George Washington. January 15, 1923. Engraved.

2c carmine

IM 130 block of 4, imperf,
ungummed **NRI**   —
Scott No. 554 var
Quantity: unique

IM 131 hz pair, imperf vrt   150.00
plate block of 6, imperf   *1,400.00*
Scott No. 554a
Quantity: n/a

IM 132 vrt pair, imperf hz   —
Scott No. 554b
Quantity: *60-100 pairs*

☛ Flat plate printed 2c stamps of the same design (Scott No. 577) were regularly issued imperforate and should not be confused with imperforate errors listed above. Faked copies of IM 131 and IM 132 can be produced from the regularly issued stamp by applying perforations.

Abraham Lincoln. February 12, 1923. Engraved.

3c dark violet

IM 133 block of 4, imperf,
ungummed **NRI**   —
Scott No. 555 var
Quantity: unique

Martha Washington. January 15, 1923. Engraved.

4c brown

IM 134 block of 4, imperf,
ungummed **NRI** —
Scott No. 556 var
Quantity: unique

IM 135 hz pair, imperf between —
Scott No. 556 var
Quantity: reportedly unique

IM 136 vrt pair, imperf hz —
Scott No. 556a
Quantity: n/a

Theodore Roosevelt. October 27, 1922. Engraved.

5c blue

IM 137 imperf pair 650.00
plate block of 6, imperf *5,000.00*
block of 4, imperf,
ungummed **NRI** —
Scott No. 557a
Quantity: 1 sheet of 100

IM 138 hz pair, imperf vrt 800.00
Scott No. 557b
Quantity: 10 pairs reported

James A. Garfield. November 20, 1922. Engraved.

6c orange

IM 139 block of 4, imperf,
ungummed **NRI** —
Scott No. 558 var
Quantity: unique

William McKinley. May 1, 1923. Engraved.

7c black

IM 140 block of 4, imperf,
ungummed **NRI** —
Scott No. 559 var
Quantity: unique

Ulysses S. Grant. May 1, 1923. Engraved.

8c olive

IM 141 block of 4, imperf,
ungummed **NRI** —
Scott No. 560 var
Quantity: unique

Thomas Jefferson. January 15, 1923. Engraved.

9c pink

IM 142 block of 4, imperf,
ungummed **NRI** —
Scott No. 561 var
Quantity: unique

James Monroe. January 15, 1923. Engraved.

10c yellow

IM 143   imperf pair, ungummed   650.00
block of 4, imperf, ungummed   1,400.00
top or bottom plate block of 6,
imperf, ungummed,   *2,750.00*
Scott No. 562b
Quantity: 2 sheets reported

Pairs with blue pencil marks sell at discounts. The two sheets reported contain large areas defaced by Bureau of Engraving & Printing inspector's blue pencil marks used to identify sheets for destruction. It is estimated that only 40-50 unmarked pairs exist.

IM 144   vrt pair, imperf hz   575.00
block of 4   —
Scott No. 562a
Quantity: 50 pairs

Rutherford Hayes. October 4, 1922. Engraved.

11c light blue

IM 145   block of 4, imperf,
ungummed   **NRI**
Scott No. 563 var   —
Quantity: unique

IM 146   vrt pair, imperf, precancelled
San Francisco, California   —
strip of 3, imperf, precancelled
San Francisco, California LRS
(82)   8,800.00
Scott No. 563d
Quantity: 1 pair nearly severed
by scissors cut and one strip of
3 reported.

Grover Cleveland. May 20, 1923. Engraved.

12c brown violet

IM 147   block of 4, imperf,
ungummed   **NRI**   —
Scott No. 564 var
Quantity: unique

IM 148   imperf pair   —
Scott No. 564b
Quantity: rare

IM 149 hz pair, imperf vrt   450.00
            block of 4, imperf vrt 900.00
            Scott No. 564a
            Quantity: *very scarce*

IM 149 is often found without gum or with government paste-up paper on reverse.

Benjamin Harrison. January 11, 1926. Engraved.

13c bluish green

IM 150 block of 4, imperf,
            ungummed **NRI**   —
            Scott No. 622 var
            Quantity: unique

American Indian. May 1, 1923. Engraved.

14c indigo

IM 151 block of 4, imperf,
            ungummed **NRI**   —
            Scott No. 565 var
            Quantity: unique

Statue of Liberty. November 11, 1922. Engraved.

15c gray

IM 152 block of 4, imperf,
            ungummed **NRI**   —
             Scott No. 566 var
             Quantity: unique

Woodrow Wilson. December 28, 1925. Engraved.

17c black

IM 153 block of 4, imperf,
            ungummed **NRI**   —
             Scott No. 623 var
             Quantity: unique

Golden Gate. May 1, 1923. Engraved.

20c carmine rose

IM 154 block of 4, imperf,
            ungummed **NRI**   —
             Scott No. 567 var
             Quantity: unique

IM 155 hz pair, imperf vrt   800.00
            block of 4, imperf vrt 1,900.00
            Scott No. 567a
            Quantity: 1/2 sheet of 100
            reported

Niagara Falls. November 11, 1922. Engraved.

25c green

IM 156 block of 4, imperf,
            ungummed **NRI**   —
             Scott No. 568 var
             Quantity: unique

IM 157 vrt pair, imperf hz   —
            block with plate No. 14063 at
            right, imperf hz   —
            Scott No. 568b
            Quantity: rare

Buffalo. March 20, 1923. Engraved.

30c brown

IM 158 block of 4, imperf,
            ungummed **NRI**   —
             Scott No. 569 var
             Quantity: unique

Tomb of the Unknown Soldier. November 11, 1922. Engraved.

  50c lavender

IM 159 block of 4, imperf,
   ungummed **NRI**   —
   Scott No. 570 var
   Quantity: unique

Lincoln Memorial. February 12, 1923. Engraved.

  $1 violet brown

IM 160 block of 4, imperf,
   ungummed **NRI**   —
   Scott. No. 571 var
   Quantity: unique

U. S. Capitol. March 20, 1923. Engraved.

  $2 blue

IM 161 block of 4, imperf,
   ungummed **NRI**   —
   Scott No. 572 var
   Quantity: unique

America. March 20, 1923. Engraved.

  $5 red & blue

IM 162 block of 4, imperf,
   ungummed **NRI**   —
   Scott No. 573 var
   Quantity: unique

  A set of ungummed, imperforate blocks of 4 (1/2c through $5) listed variously between Nos. IM 127 through IM 162, was sold at auction in 1968 for $12,200. Because it is not possible to distinguish the imperforate 10c stamp of this group from IM 143, it is not separately listed.

  The 1 1/2c, 2c, 5c, 6c and 8c denominations of this series exist imperforate with various degrees of smearing or underinking. Those which are smeared but not severely underinked might pass as stamps. In their worst form, they are virtually unrecognizable as postage stamps. They are mentioned here for the record.

SERIES OF 1923/26

Stamps of this issue are identical in design to those of the previous issue, however, are printed by rotary press and normally perforated 10. Design measures 19 by 23mm.

Theodore Roosevelt. 1925. Engraved. Perf 10.

  5c blue

IM 163 hz pair, imperf vrt   —
   Scott No. 586a
   Quantity: *very rare, possibly*
   unique

SERIES OF 1926/34

Stamps of this issue are similar in design to the two preceding issues, however, are normally perforated 11 by 10 1/2. Printed by rotary press.

Benjamin Franklin. June 10, 1927. Engraved. Perf 11x10 1/2.

  1c green

IM 164 vrt pair, imperf between 125.00
   as above, used   —
   Scott No. 632b
   Quantity: n/a

IM 165   hz pair, imperf between   —
        Scott No. 632 var
        Quantity: n/a

George Washington. December 10, 1926. Engraved. Perf 11x10 1/2.

2c carmine

IM 166   hz pair, imperf between   —
        Scott No. 634c
        Quantity: very rare

IM 167   vrt pair, imperf between   —
        Scott No. 634 var
        Quantity: very rare

William McKinley. March 24, 1927. Engraved. Perf 11x10 1/2.

7c black

IM 168   vrt pair, imperf between   100.00
        as above, used   65.00
        block of 4, imperf between hz   200.00
        Scott No. 639a
        Quantity: n/a

IM 169   vrt pair, imperf between,
        precancelled Mobile, Ala.   100.00
        Scott No. 639a
        Quantity: n/a

☛ Caution. These stamps are known with blind perfs which can be ironed out and eliminated to the naked eye, resulting in dangerous fakes. Copies lacking gum should be regarded with special caution.

Warren G. Harding. September 1, 1923. Engraved. Flat plate press. Design measures 19.25mm by 22.25mm.

2c black

IM 170   hz pair, imperf vrt   —
        Scott No. 610a
        Quantity: n/a

☛ Caution. It is possible to fabricate this error from regularly issued imperforate stamps (Scott No. 611) of the same design. Certificate of authenticity is strongly advised.

Battle of White Plains. October 18, 1926. Engraved.

2c carmine rose

IM 171   vrt pair, imperf between   *1,250.00*
        Scott No. 629a
        Quantity: very scarce

General Von Steuben. September 17, 1930. Engraved.

2c carmine rose

IM 172 imperf pair — 2,200.00
block of 4, imperf — 4,500.00
plate block of 6, imperf — —
Scott No. 689a
Quantity: 1 sheet of 100

Yorktown Sesquicentennial. October 19, 1931. Engraved.

2c carmine & black

IM 173 hz pair, imperf vrt — 1,750.00
block of 4, imperf vrt — 3,500.00
hz block of 6, imperf vrt — 4,000.00
hz center line block of 10 — *8,000.00*
bottom plate block of 10 — *8,000.00*
Scott No. 703c
Quantity: 1 sheet of 50

George Washington Bicentennial. June 16, 1932. Engraved.

3c violet

IM 174 vrt pair, imperf between — 200.00
as above, used — 225.00
Scott No. 720c
Quantity: n/a

☞ Caution. These stamps are known with blind perforations which can be ironed out and eliminated to the naked eye, resulting in dangerous fakes. Copies lacking gum should be regarded with special caution.

William Penn. October 24, 1932. Engraved.

3c violet

IM 175 vrt pair, imperf hz — —
Scott No. 724a
Quantity: n/a

General Tadeusz Kosciuszko. October 13, 1933. Engraved.

5c blue

IM 176 hz pair, imperf vrt — 1,600.00
block of 4, imperf vrt — 3,200.00
Scott No. 734a
Quantity: *1-2 sheets*

Maryland Tercentenary. May 23, 1934. Engraved.

3c carmine rose

IM 177 hz pair, imperf between — 1,000.00
Scott No. 736a
Quantity: n/a

Wisconsin Tercentenary. July 7, 1934. Engraved.

3c violet

IM 178 vrt pair, imperf hz   250.00
Scott No. 739a
Quantity: n/a

IM 179 hz pair, imperf vrt   300.00
Scott No. 739b
Quantity: n/a

NATIONAL PARK SERIES OF 1934

The stamps listed below are errors of the fully gummed, perforated set of National Parks stamps. They are similar in appearance to the Farley Special Printing which was issued fully imperforate and without gum.

Yosemite. July 16, 1934. Engraved.

1c green

IM 180 vrt pair, imperf hz, with gum   400.00
Scott No. 740a
Quantity: 16 pairs or strip of
three

☛ Caution. all known copies of this error are signed "S.A." (Spencer Anderson) on the reverse in indelible pencil. Those rubber stamped "Sloane" are fakes.

☛ Caution. It is possible to fabricate National Parks error stamps listed here from completely imperforate stamps of identical design from the Farley Special Printing of 1935 which were issued without gum. In 1940, the Bureau of Engraving & Printing offered to gum any Farley Special Printing sheets submitted by collectors. Therefore, presence of government gum on part perforate stamps is not necessarily and indication of genuiness. Certificates of authenticity are advised for part perforate error stamps which have Farley special printing counterparts.

Grand Canyon. July 24, 1934. Engraved.

2c red

IM 181 vrt pair, imperf hz, with gum   350.00
top plate block of 6, imperf hz,
with gum   *2,000.00*
Scott No. 741a
Quantity: 2-3 sheets

IM 182 hz pair, imperf vrt, with gum   400.00
Scott No. 741b
Quantity: 2-3 sheets

See note after IM 180.

Where possible, illustrations of actual error stamps were used. They are bordered in black. Where photos of errors were unavailable, illustrations of normal stamps were used. They appear without any border.

Mt. Rainier. August 3, 1934. Engraved.

3c violet

IM 183 vrt pair, imperf hz, with gum   500.00
bottom plate block of 6 with
gum, imperf hz   *1,250.00*
Scott No. 742a
Quantity: 1 sheet

☛ See note after IM 180.

Mesa Verde. September 25, 1934. Engraved.

4c brown

IM 184 vrt pair, imperf hz, with gum   750.00
Scott No. 743a
Quantity: 15 pairs

Approximately 6-9 of the 15 known pairs have brown Post Office paper
affixed to the reverse. Copies without brown paper sell for 50%-100%
premium.

Yellowstone. July 30, 1934. Engraved.

5c blue

IM 185 hz pair, imperf vrt, with gum   475.00
Scott No. 744a
Quantity: 50 pairs

☛ Caution. Fakes exist. See note after IM 180.

Acadia. October 2, 1934. Engraved.

7c black

IM 186 hz pair, imperf vrt, with gum   650.00
top plate block of 10 with gum,
imperf vrt   *1,900.00*
Scott No. 746a
Quantity: 50 pairs

☛ Caution. It is possible to fabricate the National Parks error stamps listed
above from completely imperforate stamps of identical design from the
Farley Special Printing of 1935 which were issued without gum. In 1940,
the Bureau of Engraving & Printing offered to gum any Farley Special Printing sheets submitted by collectors. Therefore, presence of government gum
on part perforate stamps is not necessarily an indication of genuineness.
Certificates of authenticity are advised when purchasing part perforate error
stamps which have Farley Special Printing counterparts.

PRESIDENTIAL SERIES OF 1938

Martha Washington. May 5, 1938. Engraved.

1 1/2c brown

IM 188 hz pair, imperf between   165.00
Scott No. 805b
Quantity: n/a

IM 189 hz pair, imperf between, pre-
cancelled St. Louis, Mo.   15.00
Scott No. 805b var
Quantity: few thousand

Thomas Jefferson. June 16, 1938. Engraved.

3c violet

IM 190 imperf pair   2,500.00
Scott No. 807c
Quantity: very rare

☞ The 3c Jefferson of the Presidential Series was counterfeited to defraud the post office. The government raided the printer and seized the stock, nevertheless, a small number of the counterfeits, fully gummed and imperforate, escaped. The counterfeits were lithographed and thus can be distinguished from engraved genuine stamps. Gum on the counterfeits does not have gum breaking ridges found on genuine stamps and the gum is much more yellow than that of genuine stamps. IM 190 should have large outer margins.

IM 191 hz pair, imperf between   575.00
Scott No. 807b
Quantity: 10 pairs reported

See note after IM 190.

Woodrow Wilson. August 29, 1938. Engraved.

$1 purple & black

IM 192 vrt pair, imperf hz   1,250.00
Scott No. 832a
Quantity: 50-100 pairs reported

IM 193 vrt pair, imperf between   2,750.00
Scott No. 832e
Quantity: very rare

Woodrow Wilson. August 31, 1954. Engraved. Printed by the dry process with smooth clear gum on somewhat thicker paper than that of the previous issue. The color also differs in having more red in the purple ink.

$1 reddish purple & black

IM 194 vrt pair, imperf hz   1,050.00
Scott No. 832d
Quantity: 1-2 sheets of 100
reported

IM 195 vrt pair, imperf between   *7,500.00*
block of 4, imperf hz between   —
Scott No. 832f
Quantity: 10 pairs

A thorough reading of the introduction will aid in using this catalogue.

NATIONAL DEFENSE SERIES OF 1940

Statue of Liberty. October 16, 1940. Engraved.

1c green

IM 196	vrt pair, imperf between Scott No. 899a Quantity: 100-200 pairs reported	350.00
IM 197	hz pair, imperf between Scott No. 899b Quantity: several thousand pairs	40.00
IM 198	hz pair, imperf between, pre- cancelled Glendale, Calif. Scott No. 899b Quantity: n/a	90.00

☛ Caution. Often encountered with blind perfs or few punched perf holes.

Anti-aircraft gun. October 16, 1940. Engraved.

2c rose carmine

IM 199	hz pair, imperf between Scott No. 900a Quantity: several thousand	50.00

☛ Caution. Often encountered with blind perfs or few punched perf holes.

Torch. October 16, 1940. Engraved.

3c violet

IM 200	hz pair, imperf between Scott No. 901a Quantity: several thousand	25.00

Mt. Palomar Observatory. August 30, 1948. Engraved.

3c blue

IM 201	vrt pair, imperf between plate block of 4, vrt imperf between Scott No. 966a Quantity: *100+* pairs, 10 plate blocks (each with 2 pairs) reported	*450.00* *900.00*

LIBERTY ISSUE OF 1954

Statue of Liberty. June 24, 1954. Engraved.

3c deep violet

IM 202   imperf pair   *1,500.00*
Scott No. 1035c
Quantity: 5-10 pairs reported

IM 203   hz pair, imperf between   *1,000.00*
Scott No. 1035d
Quantity: 5-10 pairs

BOOKLET PANE

Abraham Lincoln. July 31, 1958. Booklet pane of 6. Engraved.

4c red violet

IM 204   booklet pane of 6, imperf hz   —
Scott No. 1036a var
Quantity: *very rare, possibly unique*

IM 205   hz pair, imperf between   —
Scott No. 1036a var
Quantity: *very rare, possibly unique*

COIL STAMPS

George Washington. October 8, 1954. Engraved.

1c green

IM 206   imperf pair   *2,250.00*
Scott No. 1054b
Quantity: 13 pairs reported

Thomas Jefferson. October 22, 1954. Engraved.

2c carmine rose

IM 207   imperf pair   *325.00*
line pair, imperf   *550.00*
Scott No. 1055c
Quantity: n/a

IM 208   imperf pair, precancelled River-
dale, MD   *325.00*
line pair, imperf   —
Scott No. 1055b
Quantity: n/a

Statue of Liberty. July 20, 1954. Engraved.

3c deep violet

IM 209   imperf pair   650.00
line pair, imperf   1,250.00
used strip of 3, imperf   *660.00*
Scott No. 1057a
Quantity: 30 pairs reported

Abraham Lincoln. July 31, 1958. Engraved.

4c red violet

IM 210   imperf pair   85.00
used pair, imperf   —
line pair, imperf   *200.00*
paste up pair, imperf   —
Scott No. 1058a
Quantity: 500+ pairs reported
Exists miscut.

IM 211   imperf pair, precancelled
Seattle, Wash.   *150.00*
Scott No. 1058a
Quantity: n/a

Paul Revere. February 25, 1965. Engraved.

25c green

IM 212   imperf pair   35.00
line pair, imperf   60.00
Scott No. 1059Ac
Quantity: 1,200 pairs reported

Well centered copies are scarce.

Jose de San Martin. February 25, 1959. Engraved.

4c blue

IM 213   hz pair, imperf between   1,500.00
Scott No. 1125a
Quantity: 20 pairs reported

Ephraim McDowell. December 3, 1959. Engraved.

4c maroon

IM 214   pair, imperf hz   500.00
Scott No. 1138b
Quantity: 50+ pairs reported

IM 215   vrt pair, imperf between   500.00
Scott No. 1138a
Quantity: 210 pairs reported

Thomas G. Masaryk. March 7, 1960. Engraved.

4c blue

IM 216   vrt pair, imperf between   *1,750.00*
Scott No. 1147a
Quantity: 10 pairs

Thomas G. Masaryk. March 7, 1960. Engraved.

8c yellow, blue & red

IM 217   hz pair, imperf between   —
Scott No. 1148a
Quantity: 3 pairs reported

SEATO. May 31, 1960. Engraved.

4c blue

IM 218 vrt pair, imperf between   175.00
plate block of 4, imperf hz
between   *400.00*
Scott No. 1151a
Quantity: 100-200 pairs reported

Winslow Homer. December 15, 1962. Engraved.

4c multicolored

IM 219 hz pair, imperf between   *2,500.00*
hz pair with plate No., imperf
between LRS (84)   2,860.00
Scott No. 1207a
Quantity: 4 pairs reported

George Washington. November 23, 1962. Engraved.

5c blue gray

IM 220 hz pair, imperf between   *500.00*
hz pair (1 stamp, 1 label), im-
perf between   —
booklet pane, imperf vrt
between   —
Scott No. 1213a var
Quantity: n/a, probably very
rare

IM 220 results from miscut booklet panes and also exists se-tenant with
label containing slogan.

COIL STAMP

George Washington. November 23, 1962. Engraved.

5c blue gray

IM 221 imperf pair   275.00
line pair, imperf   —
Scott No. 1229b
Quantity: approx 50 pairs
reported

U. S. Flag. January 9, 1963. Engraved.

5c red & blue

IM 222 hz pair, imperf between   —
Scott No. 1208b
Quantity: 3-4 pairs reported

☛Caution. Pairs exist with blind perfs.

Appomattox. April 9, 1965. Engraved.

5c blue & black

IM 223 hz pair, imperf between   —
Scott No. 1182a
Quantity: *very rare*

PROMINENT AMERICANS SERIES OF 1965/1978

COIL STAMPS

Thomas Jefferson. January 12, 1968. Engraved.

1c green

IM 224 imperf pair   35.00
line pair, imperf   65.00
Scott No. 1299b
Quantity: 1,000+ pairs

Francis Parkman. November 4, 1975. Engraved.

3c violet

IM 225 imperf pair   30.00
line pair, imperf   45.00
Scott No. 1297a
Quantity: 1,000+ pairs

IM 226 imperf pair, precancelled Non-
Profit ORG CAR-RT SORT   *10.00*
line pair, imperf   *25.00*
Scott No. 1297a
Quantity: several thousand

Exists miscut.

Abraham Lincoln. May 28, 1966. Engraved.

4c black

IM 227 imperf pair   500.00
line pair, imperf   750.00
Scott No. 1303b
Quantity: 100 pairs reported

George Washington. September 8, 1966. Original design. Engraved.

5c blue

IM 228 imperf pair   *250.00*
line pair, imperf   *350.00*
used pair, imperf   *200.00*
Scott No. 1304b
Quantity: 200 pairs reported

IM 229 imperf pair, precancelled Mount
Pleasant, IA   *250.00*
as above, line pair   —
Scott No. 1304c
Quantity: n/a

Original Design   Revised Design

George Washington. Revised design. Engraved.

5c blue

IM 230 imperf pair   *650.00*
line pair, imperf   *1,250.00*
Scott No. 1304Cd
Quantity: n/a

Buying or Selling?
Consult the dealer directory at the back of the catalogue.

Franklin D. Roosevelt. December 28, 1967. Engraved. Horizontal format.

6c brown

IM 231	imperf pair	*2,000.00*
	line pair, imperf	—
	Scott No. 1298a	
	Quantity: 15 pairs reported	

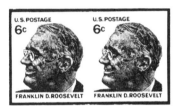

Franklin D. Roosevelt. February 28, 1968. Engraved. Vertical format.

6c brown

IM 232	imperf pair	55.00
	line pair, imperf	120.00
	Scott No. 1305a	
	Quantity: approx 1,000 pairs reported	

Dwight D. Eisenhower. August 6, 1970. Engraved.

6c grayish blue

IM 233	imperf pair	*1,000.00*
	line pair, imperf	—
	Scott No. 1401b	
	Quantity: 20-30 pairs reported	

Often with incomplete gum or without gum. Only a few pairs exist with gum. Those with gum sell for substantial premiums.

Dwight D. Eisenhower. May 10, 1971. Engraved.

8c dark claret

IM 234	imperf pair	40.00
	line pair, imperf	60.00
	paste up pair, imperf	—
	Scott No. 1402a	
	Quantity: 1,000+ pairs	

IM 235	pair, imperf between	
	Scott No. 1402c	
	Quantity: 1 pair	

Oliver Wendell Holmes. June 14, 1978. Engraved. Shiny or dry gum.

15c carmine or bright carmine

IM 236	imperf pair	30.00
	line pair, imperf	75.00
	used pair, imperf	—
	Scott No. 1305Eg	
	Quantity: 600-800 pairs	

Exists miscut.

IM 237	pair, imperf between	175.00
	Scott No. 1305Eh	
	Quantity: 150-250 pairs reported	

Eugene O'Neill. January 12, 1973. Engraved.

$1 dark violet

IM 238 imperf pair   *2,000.00*
line pair, imperf   —
Scott No. 1305Cd
Quantity: 50 pairs, 3 line pairs
reported

BOOKLET PANE

Dwight D. Eisenhower. January 28, 1972. Engraved.

8c dark claret

IM 239 block of 4 (incl label USE ZIP
CODE), imperf hz   *275.00*
Scott No. 1395d var
Quantity: n/a

BOOKLET PANE

**Oliver Wendell Holmes. June 28, 1978. Booklet pane
of 8. Engraved. Perf 10.**

15c carmine

IM 240 booklet pane of 8, imperf   *500.00*
Scott No. 1288Be
Quantity: rare

**Davy Crockett. August 17, 1967. Engraved &
lithographed.**

5c green, black & yellow

IM 241 vrt pair, imperf between   —
Scott No. 1330a
Quantity: 3-5 pairs reported

Where possible, illustrations of actual error stamps were used.
They are bordered in black. Where photos of errors were
unavailable, illustrations of normal stamps were used. They appear without any border.

FLAG SERIES OF 1968/1971

U.S. Flag. January 24, 1968. Engraved. Design 19x22mm. Perf 11.

6c red, blue & green

IM 242   vrt pair, imperf hz   135.00
Scott No. 1338c
Quantity: n/a

Most pairs are without gum. Those with full gum sell at a premium. Many offered as imperforates have traces of perforations. Check carefully.

IM 243   vrt pair, imperf between   350.00
as above, used   *125.00*
Scott No. 1338k
Quantity: n/a

U.S. Flag. August 7, 1970. Engraved. Design 18.25x21mm. Perf 11x10 1/2.

6c red, blue & green

IM 244   hz pair, imperf between   115.00
Scott No. 1338De
Quantity: n/a

Many contain clipped perfs, a normal result of trimming at the Bureau of Engraving & Printing.

U.S. Flag. May 10, 1971. Engraved. Perf 11x10 1/2.

8c red, blue & green

IM 245   imperf vertical pair   50.00
bottom plate block of 20   *700.00*
Scott No. 1338Fi
Quantity: 500 pairs reported

Pairs without gum sell at a discount. Collected in vertical pairs or blocks to distinguish from coil imperforate of similar design.

IM 246   hz pair, imperf between   *45.00*
Scott No.: 1338Fj
Quantity: 600 pairs

COIL STAMPS

U.S. Flag. May 30, 1969. Engraved.

6c red, blue & green

IM 247   imperf pair   *550.00*
paste up pair, imperf   —
Scott No. 1338Ab
Quantity: 100+ pairs

U.S. Flag. May 10, 1971. Engraved.

8c red, blue & green

IM 248   imperf pair   50.00
Scott No. 1338Gh
Quantity: 500 pairs reported

Although it is generally accepted that line pairs in the traditional sense are not created on Huck press printed stamps, pairs with coloration between stamps resembling lines exist and are collected. They sell for about double the price of regular pairs.

Walt Disney. September 11, 1968. Photogravure, by Union-Camp Corporation, Achrovure Division.

6c multicolored

IM 249   imperf pair   900.00
block of 4, imperf   —
Scott No. 1355c
Quantity: 100 pairs

IM 250   vrt pair, imperf hz   800.00
Scott No. 1355b
Quantity: 50 pairs

IM 251   hz pair, imperf between   3,100.00
Scott No. 1355e
Quantity: 5 pairs

Waterfowl Conservation. October 24, 1968. Engraved & lithographed.

6c multicolored

IM 252   vrt pair, imperf between   700.00
Scott No. 1362a
Quantity: 100+ pairs

Christmas. November 1, 1968. Engraved.

6c multicolored

IM 253   imperf pair   300.00
Scott No. 1363b
Quantity: 500 pairs

IM 254   imperf pair, untagged   450.00
Scott No. 1363d
Quantity: 250 pairs

IM 254 often occurs with mottled gum. Those with flawless gum sell at a premium.

Grandma Moses. May 1, 1969. Engraved & lithographed.

6c multicolored

IM 255   hz pair, imperf between   350.00
Scott No. 1370a
Quantity: 250 pairs reported,
see note

☛ Many pairs have faint traces of blind perfs. Frequently, perf traces can be seen only of the gum side of stamps. Pairs on cover have been reported, however, it is thought that they may have been used on cover to disguise the presence of blind perfs and, therefore, when encountered, should be examined very carefully. Of the quantity reported, it is not known how many pairs contain faint blind perfs.

Christmas. November 3, 1969. Engraved.

6c multicolored

IM 256   imperf pair   1,350.00
Scott No. 1384b
Quantity: 25 pairs reported

Christmas. November 5, 1970. Se-tenant block of 4. Photogravure, by Guilford Gravure, Inc.

6c multicolored
a) Doll Carriage
b) Toy Horse

IM 257   imperf vrt margin pair (a & b)
with plate # 31907, Washington,
DC postmark Nov. 5, 1970
LRS (76)   2,600.00

imperf vrt margin pair (a & b)
with Mail Early slogan,
Washington, DC postmark Nov.
5, 1970 LRS (74)   2,500.00
Scott No. 1416c
Quantity: each pair listed is
unique

Tom Sawyer. October 13, 1972. Engraved & lithographed.

8c multicolored

IM 258   hz pair, imperf between   2,750.00
Scott No. 1470a
Quantity: 7 pairs reported (one
of which is damaged)

George Gershwin. February 23, 1973. Photogravure.

8c multicolored

IM 259   vrt pair, imperf hz   400.00
Scott No. 1484a
Quantity: 160-200 pairs

Robinson Jeffers. August 13, 1973. Photogravure.

8c multicolored
IM 260 vrt pair, imperf hz   400.00
Scott No. 1485a
Quantity: 80-100 pairs reported

Willa Cather. September 20, 1973. Photogravure.

8c multicolored
IM 261 vrt pair, imperf hz   400.00
Scott No. 1487a
Quantity: 80-100 pairs

Lyndon B. Johnson. August 27, 1973. Photogravure.

8c multicolored
IM 262 hz pair, imperf vrt   400.00
Scott No. 1503a
Quantity: 128-160 pairs

Christmas. November 7, 1973. Photogravure.

8c multicolored

IM 263 vrt pair, imperf between   450.00
Scott No. 1508a
Quantity: 40-50 pairs

Pairs often contain a misplaced perforation in the design due to the nature of the error.

SERIES OF 1973/1974

Crossed Flags. December 8, 1973. Engraved.

10c red & blue

IM 264 hz pair, imperf between   50.00
Scott No. 1509a
Quantity: several hundred pairs

IM 265 vrt pair, imperf   850.00
block of 4, imperf   *1,600.00*
Scott No. 1509c
Quantity: 30-35 pairs

COIL STAMPS

Liberty Bell. October 1, 1974. Engraved.

6.3c reddish orange

IM 268 imperf pair   150.00
line pair, imperf   300.00
Scott No. 1518b
Quantity: 150-200 reported

IM 269 imperf pair, precancelled
Washington, DC   75.00
line pair, imperf   *100.00*
pair with gap in precancel lines,
imperf   —
paste up pair, imperf   —
Scott No. 1518c
Quantity: 300-500 pairs reported

IM 270 imperf pair, precancelled Columbus, OH   —
paste up strip of 4, imperf   —
Scott No. 1518c
Quantity: rare

IM 271 imperf pair, precancelled
Garden City, NY   —
line pair, imperf   —
Scott No. 1518c
Quantity: n/a

Jefferson Memorial. December 14, 1973. Engraved.

10c blue

IM 266 vrt pair, imperf hz   *250.00*
Scott No. 1510e
Quantity: n/a

IM 267 vrt pair, imperf between   —
Scott No. 1510f
Quantity: n/a

Occurs from miscut booklet pane.

Crossed Flags. December 8, 1973. Engraved.

10c red & blue

IM 272 imperf pair   25.00
line pair, imperf   35.00
Scott No. 1519a
Quantity: 1,000+ pairs

Refer to note after IM 248.

Where possible, illustrations of actual error stamps were used. They are bordered in black. Where photos of errors were unavailable, illustrations of normal stamps were used. They appear without any border.

Jefferson Memorial. December 14, 1973. Engraved.

10c blue

IM 273 imperf pair 35.00
line pair, imperf 75.00
paste up pair, imperf —
used imperf pair *25.00*
Scott No. 1520b
Quantity: 750 pairs
Exists miscut.

Skylab. May 14, 1974. Engraved & lithographed.

10c multicolored

IM 274 vrt pair, imperf between —
Scott No. 1529a
Quantity: n/a

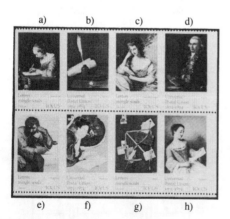

a) b) c) d)

e) f) g) h)

UPU. June 6, 1974. Se-tenant blocks of 8. Photogravure.

10c multicolored (block of 8)

a) Terboch   e) Raphael
b) Chardin   f) Hokusai
c) Gainsborough g) Peto
d) Goya   h) Liotard

IM 275 block of 8, imperf vrt *5,500.00*
Scott No. 1537b
Quantity: 8 blocks of 8 reported

Collective Bargaining. March 13, 1975. Photogravure.

10c multicolored

IM 276 imperf pair **PW** *500.00*
Scott No. 1558 var
Quantity: n/a

☛ Printers waste, refer to introduction.

Lexington & Concord. April 19, 1975. Photogravure.

10c multicolored

IM 277 vrt pair, imperf hz *550.00*
plate block of 12, imperf hz —
Scott No. 1563a
Quantity: 60-80 pairs

Paul Laurence Dunbar. May 1, 1975. Photogravure.

10c multicolored

IM 278 imperf pair *1,000.00*
plate block of 10, imperf —
Scott No. 1554a
Quantity: 15 pairs

a)

b)

Apollo-Soyuz. July 15, 1975. Se-tenant pair. Photogravure.

10c multicolored

a) Spacecraft & Globe
b) Spacecraft & Emblem

IM 279   vrt pair, imperf hz   *1,250.00*
Scott No. 1569b
Quantity: 24-36 pairs

Christmas. October 14, 1975. Photogravure.

10c multicolored

IM 280   imperf pair   125.00
plate block of 12, imperf   —
Scott No. 1579a
Quantity: several hundred pairs

Christmas. October 14, 1975. Photogravure.

10c multicolored

IM 281   imperf pair   125.00
plate block of 12, imperf   —
Scott No. 1580a
Quantity: several hundred pairs

AMERICANA SERIES OF 1975/1981

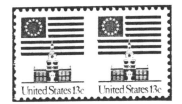

Flag & Independence Hall. November 15, 1975. Engraved. Perf 11x10 1/2.

13c red, blue & brown

IM 282   hz pair, imperf between   55.00
Scott No. 1622a
Quantity: 1,000+ pairs

IM 283   imperf vertical pair   —
block of 4, imperf   —
Scott No. 1622b
Quantity: 10-15 pairs

Flag & Independence Hall. 1981. Engraved. Perf 11.

13c red, blue & brown
IM 284   imperf vertical pair   100.00
Scott No. 1622c var
Quantity: few hundred pairs

IM 283 and IM 284 are collected in vertical pairs or blocks to distinguish them from coil imperforates of similar design.

Eagle & Shield. December 1, 1975. Photogravure.

13c multicolored

IM 285 imperf pair   40.00
block of 4, imperf   80.00
Scott No. 1596a
Quantity: few thousand

Known to exist with color shift.

IM 286   IM 287

U.S. Flag. June 30, 1978. Engraved.

15c red, blue & gray

IM 286 imperf vertical pair   20.00
block of 4, imperf   40.00
Scott No. 1597a
Quantity: 1,000+ pairs

Collected in vertical pairs or blocks to distinguish from coil imperforate of same design.

Oil Lamp. September 11, 1979. Engraved, lithographed.

50c black, orange & tan

IM 287 vrt pair, imperf hz   —
Scott No. 1609 var
Quantity: very rare

☛ Caution. Most pairs contain faint blind perfs and, therefore, do not qualify as errors. They can be deceptive. Extreme caution advised.

BOOKLET PANE

Liberty Bell. October 31, 1975. Booklet pane. Engraved.

13c brown

IM 288 vrt pair, imperf between   —
booklet pane of 7 + 1 label   —
Scott No. 1595e
Quantity: scarce

COIL STAMPS

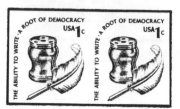

Inkwell & Quill. March 6, 1981. Engraved.

1c blue (green paper)

IM 289 imperf pair   150.00
line pair, imperf   250.00
Scott No. 1811a
Quantity: 250 pairs

Guitar. October 25, 1979. Engraved.

3.1c dark red (yellow paper)

IM 290 imperf pair   *1,000.00*
line pair, imperf   *2,000.00*
Scott No. 1613b
Quantity: 30-50 pairs, 2 line pairs

Violins. June 23, 1980. Engraved.

3.5c violet (yellow paper)

IM 291 imperf pair   275.00
line pair, imperf   *500.00*
Scott No. 1813b
Quantity: 250 pairs reported

Exists miscut.

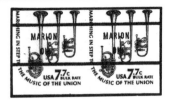

Saxhorns. November 20, 1976. Engraved.

7.7c brown (yellow paper)

IM 292 imperf pair, precancelled
Marion, OH   *500.00*
Scott No. 1614b
Quantity: 7-10 pairs reported

IM 293 imperf pair, precancelled
Washington, DC   525.00
imperf line pair, as above   —
Scott No. 1614b
Quantity: 40-50 pairs reported

Drum. April 23, 1976. Engraved.

7.9c red (yellow paper)

IM 294 imperf pair   500.00
line pair, imperf   *1,100.00*
paste up pair, imperf   —
Scott No. 1615b
Quantity: 50+ pairs reported

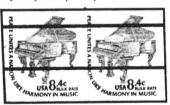

Piano. July 13, 1978. Engraved.

8.4c blue (yellow paper)

IM 295 imperf pair, precancelled bars   15.00
line pair, imperf, as above   22.50
pair with gap in precancelled
lines, imperf   —
Scott No. 1615Cf
Quantity: few thousand pairs

Exists miscut.

IM 296 pair, imperf between, precancelled bars   40.00
line pair, as above   75.00
pair, imperf between, gap in
precancelled bars   45.00
Scott No. 1615Ce
Quantity: several hundred pairs

IM 297 imperf pair, precancelled
Newark, NJ   20.00
line pair, as above   35.00
pair with gap in precancelled
lines, imperf   25.00
Scott No. 1615Cf
Quantity: n/a

Exists miscut.

IM 298 imperf pair, precancelled
Brownstown, IN   *175.00*
pair with gap in precancelled
lines, imperf   —
Scott No. 1615Cf
Quantity: n/a

IM 299 imperf pair, precancelled
Oklahoma City, OK   —
Scott No. 1615Cf
Quantity: n/a

Capitol Dome. March 5, 1976. Engraved.

9c green (gray paper)

IM 300 imperf pair   100.00
line pair, imperf   *175.00*
Scott No. 1616a
Quantity: few hundred pairs

Exists miscut in various degrees. One strip exists showing two full plate numbers at bottom and line.

IM 301   imperf pair, precancelled
      Pleasantvl, NY   *100.00*
      line pair, imperf   *225.00*
      Scott No. 1616c
      Quantity: scarce

Justice. November 4, 1977. Engraved.

10c violet (gray paper)

IM 302   imperf pair   *75.00*
      line pair, imperf   *125.00*
      Scott No. 1617b
      Quantity: few hundred pairs

Exists miscut.

Torch. April 8, 1981. Engraved.

12c red brown (gray paper)

IM 303   imperf pair   200.00
      line pair, imperf   275.00
      Scott No. 1816b
      Quantity: 250 pairs

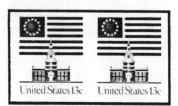

Flag & Independence Hall. November 15, 1975. Engraved.

13c red, blue & brown
IM 304   imperf pair   25.00
      line pair, imperf   35.00
      Scott No. 1625a
      Quantity: several thousand pairs

See note after IM 248.

Liberty Bell. November 25, 1975. Engraved.

13c brown
IM 305   imperf pair   35.00
      line pair, imperf   50.00
      paste up pair, imperf   —
      Scott No. 1618b
      Quantity: few thousand pairs

Exists miscut.

IM 306   pair, imperf between   *275.00*
      Scott No. 1618 var
      Quantity: scarce

U.S. Flag. June 30, 1978. Engraved

15c red, blue & gray

IM 307   imperf pair   25.00
      paste up pair, imperf   —
      Scott No. 1618Cd
      Quantity: several thousand pairs

IM 308   pair, imperf between   175.00
      Scott No. 1618Ce
      Quantity: 50-100 pairs

a)   b)   c)

The Spirit of '76. January 1, 1976. Se-tenant strip of 3. Photogravure.

13c multicolored

a) *Drummer boy*
b) *Adult drummer*
c) *Fifer*

IM 309	imperf strip of 3 (a-c)	1,750.00
	plate block of 12, imperf	—
	imperf vertical pair (c)	1,250.00
	imperf single (c), white border all around	950.00
	Scott No. 1631b, c	
	Quantity: 3 sheets of 50 yielding 45 possible strips of 3 and 15 others as singles or pairs.	

BICENTENNIAL SOUVENIR SHEETS

A variety of errors of perforation and color exist for this series. Some sheets contain multiple errors. Only those which exist imperforate, although they may also contain color(s) omitted errors, are listed here. Refer to the color(s) omitted section of the catalogue for other varieties. Because the souvenir sheets were sold in sets in envelopes, new discoveries are made occasionally. Those listed below are known at press time, other varieties may exist. Gaps in the numbering system exist to accommodate possible future listings.

Surrender at Yorktown. May 29, 1976. Souvenir sheet of 5 stamps. Lithographed.

13c multicolored

IM 310	imperf souvenir sheet, untagged, tied by postmark (5/29/76) to first day display card LRS (79) Scott No. 1868h Quantity: 1-2 reported	1,800.00
IM 311	imperf souvenir sheet, untagged, yellow (USA 13c) omitted on 1st stamp, brown (USA 13c) omitted on 2nd & 5th stamps, & orange (USA 13c) omitted on 3rd & 4th stamps, with 5/29/75 Philadelphia, PA precancel postmark LRS (76) Scott No. 1686 var Quantity: 1-2 reported	1,600.00
IM 312	imperf souvenir sheet, untagged, brown (USA 13c) omitted on 2nd stamp, orange (USA 13c) omitted on 3rd & 4th stamps, with 5/29/76 Philadelphia, PA first day precancel postmark LRS (86) Scott No. 1686f Quantity: 1-2 reported	1,980.00
IM 313	imperf souvenir sheet, yellow (USA 13c) omitted on 1st & 5th stamps Scott No. 1686 var Quantity: *possibly unique*	—

Declaration of Independence. May 29, 1976. Souvenir sheet of 5. Lithographed.

18c multicolored

| IM 316 | imperf souvenir sheet, brown (USA 18c) omitted on 1st & 3rd stamps, orange (USA 18c) omitted on 2nd & 5th stamps, and yellow (USA 13c) omitted on 4th stamp Scott No. 1687k Quantity: possibly unique | — |

Washington Crossing the Delaware. May 29, 1976, Souvenir sheet of 5. Lithographed.

24c multicolored

IM 317   imperf souvenir sheet, untagged
LRS (86)   1,540.00
Scott No. 1688j
Quantity: *very rare*

IM 318   imperf souvenir sheet, untagged,
blue (USA 24c) omitted from
1st stamp, light blue (USA 24c)
omitted from 2nd & 3rd stamps,
and white (USA 24c) omitted
from 4th & 5th stamps LRS
(76)   2,200.00
Scott No. 1688f
Quantity: *unique*

Washington at Valley Forge. May 29, 1976. Souvenir sheet of 5. Lithographed.

31c multicolored

IM 322   imperf souvenir sheet, untagged,
tied by 5/29/76 Philadelphia,
PA precancel postmark to first
day display card LRS (78)   1,200.00
Scott No. 1689k
Quantity: *unique*

IM 323   imperf souvenir sheet, untagged,
gray (USA 31c) omitted on 1st
& 3rd stamps, brown (USA
31c) omitted on 2nd & 4th
stamps, and white (USA 31c)
omitted on 5th stamp LRS (87)   1,870.00
Scott No. 1689f
Quantity: 2-4 reported

IM 324   imperf souvenir sheet, untagged,
gray (USA 31c) omitted on 1st
& 3rd stamps, white (USA 31c)
omitted on 5th stamp LRS (81)   1,760.00
Scott No. 1689n
Quantity: *unique*

IM 325   imperf souvenir sheet, untagged,
brown (USA 31c) omitted on
2nd & 4th stamps, white (USA
31c) omitted on 5th stamp   —
Scott No. 1689p
Quantity: *very rare*

a)   b)
c)   d)

Olympics. July 16, 1976. Se-Tenant blocks of 4. Photogravure.

13c multicolored
  a) Diver
  b) Skier
  c) Runner
  d) Skater

IM 329   imperf block of 4 (a-d)   1,100.00
plate block of 12, imperf   —
Zip block of 4, imperf   —
imperf pair (a-b) or (c-d)   400.00
Scott No. 1698b
Quantity: 60-80 blocks of 4
reported

Clara Maass. August 18, 1976. Photogravure.

13c multicolored

IM 330 hz pair, imperf vrt   575.00
Scott No. 1699a
Quantity: 40-80 pairs reported

Christmas. October 27, 1976. Photogravure.

13c multicolored

IM 331 imperf pair   125.00
block of 4, imperf   250.00
plate block of 12, imperf   —
Scott No. 1701a
Quantity: few hundred pairs

CHRISTMAS 1976

Stamps of the following design exist in two varieties, each printed by a different press. The second has more gray and is washed out in overall appearance. The varieties also can be can be distinguished under UV light. On Type I the entire stamp is completely tagged. Type II is tagged with rectangles that cover only the design area.

Christmas. October 27, 1976. Photogravure.

13c multicolored, type I

IM 332 imperf pair   125.00
plate block of 12, imperf   —
Scott No. 1702a
Quantity: few hundred pairs

13c multicolored, type II

IM 333 imperf pair   125.00
plate strip of 20, imperf   —
Scott No. 1703a
Quantity: 100 pairs reported

IM 334 vrt pair, imperf between   *1,000.00*
Scott No. 1703b
Quantity: 40-60 pairs

Washington at Princeton. January 3, 1977. Photogravure.

13c multicolored

IM 335 hz pair, imperf vrt   450.00
Scott No. 1704a
Quantity: n/a

a) b) c) d)

Pueblo Art. April 13, 1977. Se-Tenant blocks or strips of 4. Photogravure.

13c multicolored
    a) Hopi pottery
    b) Acoma pottery
    c) Zia pottery
    d) San Ildefonso pottery

IM 336 block of 4 (a-d), imperf vrt   2,600.00
strip of 4 (a-d), imperf vrt   2,600.00
Scott No. 1709b
Quantity: 16 blocks of 4, 4
strips of 4 reported

Sheets of the Pueblo Pottery stamp were arranged so that the four designs are se-tenant (a-b-c-d) in a row. Additionally, rows alternate so that it is possible for the four designs to appear in a se-tenant block of four.

Spirit of St. Louis. May 20, 1977. Photogravure.

13c multicolored

IM 337 imperf pair   1,750.00
Scott No. 1710a
Quantity: 60-75 pairs reported

Colorado. May 21, 1977. Photogravure.

13c multicolored

IM 338 hz pair, imperf vrt   750.00
Scott No. 1711a
Quantity: 35 pairs

a)   b)

c)   d)

Butterflies. June 6, 1977. Se-tenant blocks of 4. Photogravure.

13c multicolored

    a) Swallowtail
    b) Checkerspot
    c) Dogface
    d) Orange-Tip

IM 339 block of 4 (a-d), imperf hz,
plate numbers at left LRS (86)   12,650.00
block of 4 (a-d), imperf hz,
perfs slightly in at lower right
LRS (80)   11,000.00
Scott No. 1712-15
Quantity: the 2 blocks as listed

Christmas. October 21, 1977. Photogravure.

13c multicolored

IM 340 imperf pair   100.00
plate block of 20, imperf   —
Scott No. 1729a
Quantity: 1,000+ pairs

Christmas. October 21, 1977. Photogravure.

13c multicolored

IM 341 imperf pair   300.00
Scott No. 1730a
Quantity: n/a

a)   b)

Captain James Cook. January 20, 1978. Printed in sheets of 50 arranged so that each half sheet contains 25 stamps of the same design. Five se-tenant pairs exist at the center of each sheet. Engraved.

13c dark blue (a), green (b)

    a) Captain Cook
    b) Ships at anchor

IM 342 se-tenant pair (a-b), imperf
between   4,000.00
Scott No. 1732b
Quantity: fewer than 5 pairs
reported

b)

IM 343 vrt pair (b), imperf hz —
Scott No. 1733a
Quantity: very rare

☛Caution. Pairs of the Captain Cook design exist with blind perforations giving the appearance of being imperforate.

Indian Head Penny. January 11, 1978. Engraved.

13c brown & greenish (ochre paper)

IM 344 hz pair, imperf vrt 325.00
Scott No. 1734a
Quantity: 300-375 pairs

Eagle & A. May 22, 1978. Photogravure.

A (15c) orange

IM 345 imperf pair 85.00
plate block of 4, imperf 200.00
Scott No. 1735a
Quantity: few hundred pairs

IM 346 vrt pair, imperf hz 400.00
plate block of 4, imperf hz —
Scott No. 1735b
Quantity: 15-20 pairs reported

COIL STAMP

Eagle & A. May 27, 1978. Engraved.

A (15c) orange
IM 347 imperf pair 100.00
line pair, imperf —
Scott No. 1743a
Quantity: 125-200 pairs

BOOKLET PANE

Eagle & A. May 22, 1978. Engraved.

A (15c) orange
IM 348 vrt pair, imperf between 700.00
Scott No. 1736a var
Quantity: very rare

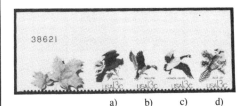

a)   b)   c)   d)

CAPEX. June 10, 1978. Souvenir sheet of 8. Engraved and lithographed.

13c multicolored

a) Cardinal	e) Moose
b) Mallard	f) Chipmunk
c) Canada Goose	g) Red Fox
d) Blue Jay	h) Raccoon

IM 349   strip of 4 (a-d), imperf vrt and
at top LRS (81)   *10,400.00*
Scott No. 1757 var
Quantity: 2 strips of 4 reported

IM 350   strip of 4 (e-h), imperf vrt LRS
(79)   *3,000.00*
as above, in souvenir sheet LRS
(86)   *4,180.00*
Scott No. 1757 var
Quantity: 6 strips of 4, including those within souvenir
sheets.

Roses. July 11, 1978. Booklet pane. Engraved.

15c green, orange & rose

IM 351   booklet pane of 8, imperf   *4,000.00*
Scott No. 1737b
Quantity: 2 panes reported

a) b) c) d)

**Trees. October 9, 1978. Se-tenant blocks of 4.
Photogravure.**

15c multicolored

a) Giant Sequoia
b) White Pine
c) White Oak
d) Gray Birch

IM 352   block of 4 (a-d), imperf hz   —
Scott No. 1767b
Quantity: unique

Christmas Madonna. October 18, 1978. Photogravure.

15c multicolored

IM 353   imperf pair   150.00
Scott No. 1768a
Quantity: 250-400 pairs

**Christmas Hobby Horse. October 18, 1978. Pho-
togravure.**

15c multicolored

IM 354   imperf pair   125.00
plate block of 12, imperf   —
Scott No. 1769a
Quantity: 200-300 pairs

IM 355   vrt pair, imperf hz   *2,000.00*
Scott No. 1769b
Quantity: 4 pairs or strips of 3
reported

   Contains traces of blind vertical perfs which may make it appear to be completely imperforate.

Martin Luther King. January 13, 1979. Photogravure.

13c multicolored

IM 356   imperf pair   *750.00*
Scott No. 1771a
Quantity: n/a

☞ Caution. Many exist with blind perfs.

Where possible, illustrations of actual error stamps were used. They are bordered in black. Where photos of errors were unavailable, illustrations of normal stamps were used. They appear without any border.

a)   b)

c)   d)

Folk Art. April 19, 1979. Se-tenant blocks of 4. Photogravure.

15c multicolored

   a) *Coffeepot*
   b) *Tea Caddy*
   c) *Sugar Bowl*
   d) *Coffeepot*

IM 357   block of 4 (a-d), imperf hz   *3,000.00*
block of 6, imperf hz   —
Scott No. 1778b
Quantity: 1 sheet consisting of 4
blocks of 4 and 4 blocks of 6
reported

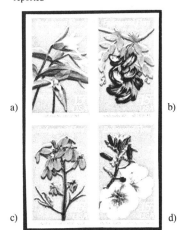

a)   b)

c)   d)

Endangered Flora. June 7, 1979. Se-tenant blocks of 4. Photogravure.

15c multicolored

   a) *Persistent Trillium*
   b) *Hawaiian Wild Broadbean*
   c) *Contra Costa Wallflower*
   d) *Antioch Dunes Evening Primrose*

IM 358   block of 4 (a-d), imperf   *750.00*
plate block of 12, imperf   —
Scott No. 1783b
Quantity: 100 blocks of 4, 50
pairs

Seeing for Me. June 15, 1979. Photogravure.

15c multicolored

IM 359	imperf pair	500.00
	Scott No. 1787a	
	Quantity: 100 pairs	

IM 360	**IM 361**	**IM 362**

John Paul Jones. September 23, 1979. Photogravure by J. W. Fergusson & Sons. Two perforation varieties; Type I perf 11x12, Type II perf 11x11.

15c multicolored

IM 360	imperf pair **PW**	*150.00*
	Scott No. 1789 var	
	Quantity: n/a	

☞ Printers waste, refer to introduction.

IM 361	vrt pair Type I, perf 12 vrt, im-perf hz	210.00
	as above, Zip block of 4	—
	Scott No. 1789c	
	Quantity: 60-100 pairs	

IM 362	vrt pair Type II, perf 11 vrt, imperf hz	150.00
	as above, plate block of 10	—
	as above, Zip block of 4	—
	Scott No. 1789d	
	Quantity: 100-140 pairs	

The fully perforated version of this issue exists in a third variety, perf 12.

a)   b)

c)   d)

Summer Olympics. September 5, 1979. Se-tenant blocks of 4. Photogravure.

15c multicolored

a) Running
b) Swimming
c) Rowing
d) Horse Jumping

IM 363	block of 4 (a-d), imperf	2,000.00
	plate block of 12, imperf	—
	Zip block of 4, imperf	—
	vrt pair (a & c), imperf	575.00
	vrt pair (b & d), imperf	575.00
	Scott No. 1794b	
	Quantity: 20 blocks of 4, 10 pairs	

Christmas Madonna. October 18, 1979. Photogravure.

15c multicolored

IM 364	imperf pair	100.00
	Scott No. 1799a	
	Quantity: 300-500 pairs	

IM 365	vrt pair, imperf between	*2,500.00*
	Scott No. 1799 var	
	Quantity: *very rare, possibly unique*	

A thorough reading of the introduction will aid in using this catalogue.

IM 366 vrt pair, imperf hz   *1,000.00*
Scott No. 1799b
Quantity: 10-15 pairs reported

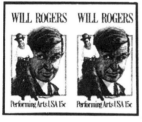

Will Rogers. November 4, 1979. Photogravure.

15c multicolored

IM 367 imperf pair   *275.00*
Scott No. 1801a
Quantity: several hundred pairs

Benjamin Bannecker. February 15, 1980. Photogravure.

15c multicolored

IM 368 imperf pair **PW**   *75.00*
Scott No. 1804 var
Quantity: n/a

☛ Printers waste, refer to introduction.

IM 369 hz pair, imperf vrt   *750.00*
Scott No. 1804a
Quantity: 25 pairs reported

COIL STAMP

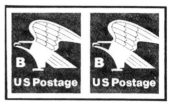

Eagle & B. March 15, 1980. Engraved.

B (18c) violet

IM 370 imperf pair   *85.00*
line pair, imperf   100.00
paste up pair, imperf   —
Scott No. 1820a
Quantity: 300-400 pairs

Emily Bissell. May 31, 1980. Engraved.

15c red & black
IM 371 vrt pair, imperf hz   *500.00*
Scott No. 1823a
Quantity: 40 pairs

Veterans Administration. July 21, 1980. Photogravure.

15c red & blue

IM 372 hz pair, imperf vrt   *650.00*
Scott No. 1825a
Quantity: 50 pairs

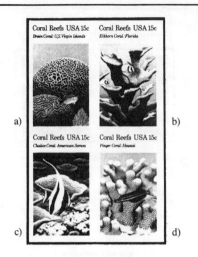

a) b) c) d)

Coral Reefs. August 26, 1980. Se-tenant in blocks of 4. Photogravure.

15c multicolored

a) Brain Coral
b) Elkhorn Coral
c) Chalice Coral
d) Finger Coral

IM 373   block of 4 (a-d), imperf   1,650.00
any pair, imperf   375.00
Scott No. 1830b
Quantity: 60-80 blocks of 4,
30-40 pairs

IM 374   block of 4 (a-d), imperf
between vrt   —
Scott No. 1830c
Quantity: 2 blocks of 4 reported

IM 375   block of 4 (a-d), imperf vrt   *2,750.00*
Scott No. 1830d
Quantity: 2-3 blocks reported

☛ Caution. Blind perfs may exist. Examine carefully.

Organized Labor. September 1, 1980. Photogravure.

15c multicolored

IM 376   imperf pair   550.00
Zip block of 4, imperf   —
Scott No. 1831a
Quantity: 100-150 pairs reported

Learning Never Ends. September 12, 1980. Photogravure.

15c multicolored

IM 377   vrt pair, imperf vrt   400.00
as above, plate block of 8   —
Scott No. 1833a
Quantity: approx 100 pairs

Christmas Madonna. October 31, 1980. Photogravure.

15c multicolored

IM 378   imperf pair   90.00
Scott No. 1842a
Quantity: 1,000+ pairs

Copies without gum sell for substantial discounts.

Christmas Drum. October 31, 1980. Photogravure.

15c multicolored

IM 379   imperf pair   90.00
as above, plate block of 20   *1,000.00*
Scott No. 1843a
Quantity: 1,000+ pairs

GREAT AMERICANS SERIES OF 1980

Dorothea Dix. September 23, 1983. Engraved.

1c black

IM 380 imperf pair — 325.00
Scott No. 1844a
Quantity: 50 pairs

Sinclair Lewis. March 21, 1985. Engraved.

14c gray green

IM 385 hz pair, imperf between — 15.00
Scott No. 1856b
Quantity: several thousand pairs

IM 386 vrt pair, imperf hz — 200.00
Scott No. 1856a
Quantity: 200-250 pairs reported

IM 387 vrt pair, imperf between — 1,000.00
Scott No. 1856c
Quantity: 10 pairs reported

Grenville Clark. May 20, 1985. Engraved.

39c bright purple

IM 393 vrt pair, imperf hz — 600.00
strip of 3, imperf hz — 800.00
Scott No. 1867a
Quantity: 20-40 pairs reported

Horizontal folds between stamps exist on some copies of this error.

IM 394 vrt pair, imperf between — —
Scott No. 1867 var
Quantity: 3 pairs reported

Flag & Grain. April 24, 1981. Engraved.

18c red, blue & brown

IM 400 imperf pair — 100.00
Scott No. 1890a
Quantity: several hundred pairs

COIL STAMP

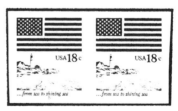

Flag & Seashore. April 24, 1981. Engraved.

18c red, blue & brown

IM 401 imperf pair — 20.00
imperf strip with plate No. 2 — 135.00
imperf strip with plate No. 5 — 60.00
Scott No. 1891a
Quantity: 1,000+ pairs

Plate number prices are for strips of 3, larger strips sell for premiums.

Buying or Selling?
Consult the dealer directory at the back of the catalogue.

BOOKLET PANE

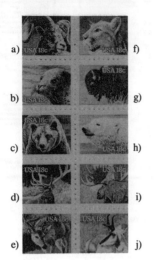

a) f)
b) g)
c) h)
d) i)
e) j)

American Wildlife. March 15, 1981. Se-tenant booklet pane of 10. Engraved.

18c dark brown

a) *Bighorn Sheep*	f) *Cougar*
b) *Seal*	g) *Bison*
c) *Bear*	h) *Polar Bear*
d) *Elk*	i) *Moose*
e) *Deer*	j) *Pronghorn Antelope*

IM 402 booklet pane of 10, imperf vrt   —
Scott No. 1819a var
Quantity: very rare

Flag & Mountains se-tenant with numeral "6" in Circle of Stars. April 24, 1981. Engraved.

6c blue & red, Numeral in Circle of Stars
18c red, blue & purple, Flag over Mountains

IM 403 booklet pane of 8 (6c & 18c),
imperf vrt   80.00
Scott No. 1893b
Quantity: 700-800 booklet panes

COIL STAMP

Eagle & C. October 11, 1981. Photogravure.
C (20c) brown

IM 404 imperf pair   *650.00*
line strip of 4, imperf   —
Scott No. 1947a
Quantity: 25-40 pairs

The gum along the edges of most pairs appears to have been slightly disturbed by moisture.

U.S. Flag. December 17, 1981. Engraved.
20c red, blue & black

IM 405 imperf vertical pair   20.00
block of 4, imperf   40.00
Scott No. 1894a
Quantity: 1,000+

Collected in vertical pairs or blocks to distinguish it from coil imperforate of the same design.

IM 406 vrt pair, imperf hz   —
Scott No. 1894b
Quantity: very scarce

COIL STAMP

U.S. Flag. December 17, 1981. Engraved.
20c red, blue & black

IM 407 imperf pair 7.50
strip with plate No. 8, imperf 50.00
strip with plate No. 9, imperf 90.00
strip with plate No. 10 .... 125.00
strip with plate No. 13 .... 125.00
Scott No.: 1895a
Quantity: few thousand pairs

Exists miscut. Prices are for plate strips of 3, strips of 5 or larger sell for 50%-100% premiums.

IM 408 pair, imperf between .... —
Scott No. 1895d
Quantity: 4 pairs reported

BOOKLET PANE

Bighorn Sheep. January 8, 1982. Engraved.

20c gray blue

IM 409 booklet pane of 10, imperf vrt
between 125.00
Scott No. 1949b
Quantity: n/a

TRANSPORTATION SERIES OF 1982 COIL STAMPS

Locomotive. May 20, 1982. Engraved.
2c black

IM 410 imperf pair 100.00
imperf strip with plate No. 3 .... *450.00*
imperf strip with plate No. 4 .... —
imperf strip with plate No. 8 .... *350.00*
imperf strip with plate No. 10 .... *350.00*
Scott No. 1897Ae
Quantity: 500+ pairs

Prices are for plate strips of 6 with plate numbers & lines.

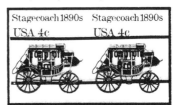

Stagecoach. August 19, 1982. Engraved.

4c reddish brown

IM 411 imperf pair, precancelled 2 bars
& NON-PROFIT Org. 450.00
imperf strip with plate No. 5 .... —
imperf strip with plate No. 6 .... —
imperf pair, gap in bars .... —
Scott No. 1898Ac
Quantity: 50-75 pairs

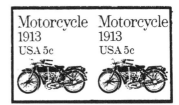

Motorcycle. October 10, 1983. Engraved.

5c gray green

IM 413 imperf pair .... —
Scott No. 1900a
Quantity: 1,000+ pairs

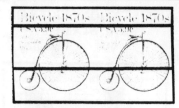

Bicycle. May 17, 1982. Engraved.

5.9c blue

IM 414   imperf pair, precancelled 2 bars   *185.00*
imperf strip with plate No. 3   —
imperf strip with plate No. 4   —
imperf pair, gap in bars   —
Scott No. 1901b
Quantity: 480 pairs reported

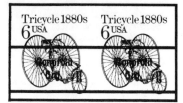

Tricycle. May 6, 1985. Engraved.

6c red brown

IM 416   imperf pair, precancelled NON-
PROFIT Org.   *200.00*
imperf strip with plate No.   —
Scott No: 2126b
Quantity: *new, 250 pairs
reported*

Mail Wagon. December 15, 1982. Engraved

9.3c brownish purple

IM 418   imperf pair, precancelled 2 bars   125.00
imperf strip with plate No. 1   —
imperf strip with plate No. 2   —
as above, gap in bars   —
Scott No. 1903b
Quantity: 250 pairs reported

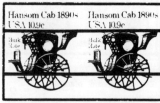

Oil Wagon. April 18, 1985. Engraved.

10.1c slate blue

IM 420   imperf pair, precancelled 2 bars
& BULK RATE   —
imperf strip of 6 with plate No. 1   —
Scott No. 2130a var
Quantity: 350-500 pairs reported

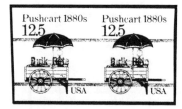

Hansom Cab. March 26, 1982. Engraved.

10.9c purple

IM 421   imperf pair, precancelled 2 bars   *160.00*
imperf strip with plate No. 1   —
imperf strip with plate No. 2   —
imperf strip with plate No. 3   —
imperf pair, gap in bars   —
Scott No. 1904b
Quantity: *250 pairs reported*

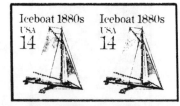

Pushcart. April 18, 1985. Engraved.

12.5c dark olive green

IM 423   imperf pair, precancelled bars &
BULK RATE   *80.00*
imperf strip of 6 with plate No. 1   —
imperf pair, gap in precancel   —
Scott No. 2132b
Quantity: 600 pairs reported

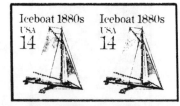

Iceboat. March 23, 1985. Engraved.

14c light blue

IM 425   imperf pair   70.00
imperf strip with plate No.1   *475.00*
imperf strip with plate No.2   *475.00*
Scott No. 2134a
Quantity: 350 pairs reported

Prices are for plate strips of 6.

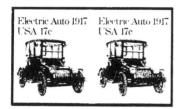

Electric Auto. June 25, 1982. Engraved.

17c blue

IM 427 imperf pair   150.00
imperf strip with plate No. 4   —
used pair, imperf   —
Scott No. 1906b
Quantity: 200 pairs reported

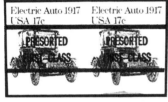

IM 428 imperf pair, precancelled 2 bars
& PRESORTED FIRST- CLASS   300.00
as above, gap in precancel   —
imperf strip with plate No.   —
Scott No.: 1906c
Quantity: 80 pairs reported

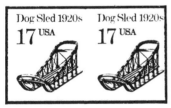

Dog Sled. August 20, 1986. Engraved.

17c blue

IM 429 imperf pair   —
imperf strip with plate No.   —
Scott No. 2135 var
Quantity: *new, 50 pairs
reported*

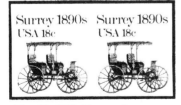

Surrey. May 15, 1982. Engraved.

18c dark brown

IM 430 imperf pair   *110.00*
imperf strip with plate No. 2   —
imperf strip with plate No. 8   —
imperf strip with plate No. 9   —
imperf strip with plate No. 10   —
paste up strip, imperf   —
Scott No. 1907a
Quantity: 400-500 pairs reported

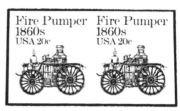

Fire Pumper. December 10, 1982. Engraved.

20c red

IM 432 imperf pair   95.00
imperf pair or strip with plate
No.   —
Scott No.: 1908a
Quantity: several hundred pairs

Plate numbers 1, 2, 3, 4, 5, 15 & 16 have been reported. Plate number pairs and strips of various length exist. Generally, longer strips command greater premiums. Exists miscut.

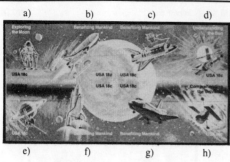

Space Achievement. May 21, 1981. Photogravure.

18c multicolored

a) *Exploring the Moon*
b) *Space Shuttle*
c) *Space Shuttle Launching Satellite*
d) *Understanding the Sun*
e) *Probing the Planets*
f) *Space Shuttle Blasting Off*
g) *Space Shuttle with Landing Gear Down*
h) *Comprehending the Universe*

IM 440 block of 8 (a-g), imperf   *8,000.00*
plate block of 8 (a-g), imperf
LRS (81)   *12,100.00*
Zip block of 8 (a-g), imperf
LRS (81)   *17,600.00*
Scott No. 1919b
Quantity: 4-6 blocks of 8
reported

Year of the Disabled. June 29, 1981. Photogravure.

18c multicolored

IM 441 vrt pair, imperf hz   *2,500.00*
Scott No. 1925a
Quantity: 10 pairs reported

Beat Alcoholism. August 19, 1981. Engraved.

18c black & blue

IM 442 imperf pair   350.00
Scott No. 1927a
Quantity: n/a

Frederic Remington. October 9, 1981. Engraved.

18c brown, dark green & gray

IM 443 vrt pair, imperf between   325.00
Scott No. 1934a
Quantity: 200 pairs reported

☛ Caution. Pairs or strips of 3 exist with blind perfs.

Christmas Madonna. October 28, 1981. Photogravure.

Non-denominated (20c) multicolored

IM 444 imperf pair   175.00
Scott No. 1939a
Quantity: few hundred pairs

Christmas Toys. October 28, 1981. Photogravure.

Non-denominated (20c) multicolored

IM 445 imperf pair   200.00
Scott No. 1940a
Quantity: 200-400 pairs

IM 446 vrt pair, imperf hz —
Scott No. 1940b
Quantity: 100-150 pairs

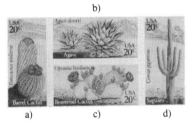

Cactus. December 11, 1981. Se-tenant blocks of 4. Engraved, lithographed.

20c multicolored

a) *Barrel Cactus*
b) *Agave*
c) *Beavertail Cactus*
d) *Saguaro*

IM 447 vrt pair (d only), imperf hz 2,500.00
Scott No. 1945 var
Quantity: 5 reported

Love. February 1, 1982. Photogravure.

20c multicolored

IM 448 imperf pair 300.00
plate block of 4, imperf 700.00
Scott No. 1951b
Quantity: 200-250 pairs reported

Horizontal pairs usually sell for more than vertical pairs.

State Birds & Flowers. April 14, 1982. Issued in se-tenant sheets of 50. Photogravure.

20c multicolored.

IM 449 sheet of 50, imperf —
Scott No. 2002d
Quantity: unique

Netherlands/USA. April 20, 1983. Photogravure.

20c multicolored

IM 450 imperf pair 450.00
Scott No. 2003a
Quantity: 94 pairs reported

Consumer Education. April 27, 1982. Engraved.

20c light blue

IM 451 imperf pair 100.00
imperf pair or strip with plate
No. —
Scott No. 2005a
Quantity: few hundred pairs

Plate numbers 1, 2, & 3 reported. Exists miscut.

America's Libraries. July 13, 1982. Engraved.

20c red & black

IM 452 vrt pair, imperf hz   *500.00*
Scott No.: 2015a
Quantity: 100-120 pairs

Touro Synagogue. August 22, 1982. Photogravure.

20c multicolored

IM 453 imperf pair   *600.00*
Scott No. 2017a
Quantity: 25 pairs

Ponce de Leon. October 2, 1982. Photogravure.

20c multicolored

IM 454 imperf pair   *800.00*
Scott No. 2024a
Quantity: 32 pairs reported

Where possible, illustrations of actual error stamps were used. They are bordered in black. Where photos of errors were unavailable, illustrations of normal stamps were used. They appear without any border.

Christmas Puppy & Kitten. November 3, 1982. Photogravure.

13c multicolored

IM 455 imperf pair   —
Scott No. 2025a
Quantity: 75-100 pairs reported

Some pairs are faulty. They sell for less than sound pairs.

Christmas Madonna. October 28, 1982. Photogravure.

20c multicolored

IM 456 imperf pair   200.00
Scott No.: 2026a
Quantity: *50-75+* pairs reported

IM 457 hz, imperf vrt   *1,375.00*
Scott No. 2026 var
Quantity: 3-6 pairs reported

a)   b)

c)   d)

Christmas Winter Scenes. October 28, 1982. Se-tenant blocks of 4. Photogravure.

20c multicolored

a) *Sledding*
b) *Snowman*
c) *Skating*
d) *Christmas tree*

IM 458 block of 4 (a-d), imperf   *1,750.00*
Scott No. 2030b
Quantity: n/a

IM 459 block of 4 (a-d), imperf hz   —
Scott No. 2030c
Quantity: n/a

c)

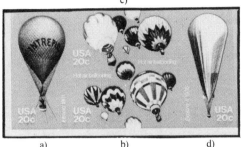

a)   b)   d)

Balloons. March 31, 1983. Se-tenant blocks of 4. Photogravure.

    20c multicolored

> a) *Intrepid*
> b) *Hot Air Ballooning*
> c) *Hot Air Ballooning*
> d) *Explorer II*

IM 460 block of 4, imperf   *2,500.00*
       copyright block of 4, imperf   *2,100.00*
Scott No. 2035b
Quantity: 10 blocks of 4

Civilian Conservation Crops. April 5, 1983. Photogravure.

    20c multicolored

IM 461 imperf pair   *2,400.00*
Scott No. 2037a
Quantity: 25 pairs

Volunteer Lend A Hand. April 30, 1983. Engraved.

    20c black & red

IM 462 imperf pair   *1,250.00*
Scott No. 2039a
Quantity: 25 pairs reported

These stamps have an underinked appearance.

Scott Joplin. June 9, 1983. Photogravure.

    20c multicolored

IM 463 imperf pair   *550.00*
Scott No. 2044a
Quantity: 25-50 pairs reported

Christmas Santa Claus. October 28, 1983. Photogravure.

    20c multicolored

IM 464 imperf pair   180.00
Scott No. 2064a
Quantity: 100-150 pairs

Buying or Selling?
Consult the dealer directory at the back of the catalogue.

Love. January 31, 1984. Photogravure.

20c multicolored

IM 465 hz pair, imperf vrt   *275.00*
Scott No. 2072a
Quantity: 100-150 pairs

Carter G. Woodson. January 31, 1984. Photogravure.

20c multicolored

IM 466 hz pair, imperf vrt   —
Scott No. 2073a
Quantity: 25 pairs reported

Preserving Wetlands. July 2, 1984. Engraved.

20c blue

IM 468 hz pair, imperf vrt   *450.00*
Zip block, imperf   —
Scott No. 2092a
Quantity: 56 pairs reported

Smokey. August 13, 1984. Photogravure.

20c multicolored

IM 469 hz pair, imperf between   *450.00*
plate block of 4, vrt imperf
between   —
Scott No. 2096a
Quantity: n/a

IM 470 vrt pair, imperf between   *275.00*
Scott No. 2096b
Quantity: 160-200 pairs

IM 471 block of 4, imperf hz & vrt (internally) between   *3,000.00*
Scott No. 2096c
Quantity: 6 blocks of 4 (including 1 faulty block)

Roberto Clemente. August 17, 1984. Photogravure.

20c multicolored

IM 472 hz pair, imperf vrt   *1,000.00*
hz strip of 3, vrt imperf   —
Scott No. 2097a
Quantity: 20 pairs, 3 strips of 3
reported

Family Unity. October 1, 1984. Photogravure.

20c multicolored

IM 473 hz pair, imperf vrt   *750.00*
Scott No. 2104a
Quantity: 25 pairs reported

Hispanic Americans. October 31, 1984. Photogravure.

20c multicolored

IM 474 vrt pair, imperf hz   *1,500.00*
Scott No. 2103a
Quantity: 20 pairs reported

Eagle & D. February 1, 1985. Photogravure.

D (22c) green

IM 475 imperf vrt pair   40.00
block of 4, imperf   80.00
Zip block of 4, imperf   100.00
copyright block of 4, imperf 100.00
Scott No.: 2111a
Quantity: 1,000+

IM 476 vrt pair, imperf hz   —
Scott No. 2111 var
Quantity: n/a

COIL STAMP

Eagle & D. February 1, 1985. Photogravure.

D (22c) green

IM 477 imperf pair   40.00
imperf pair or strip with plate No. 1 —
imperf pair or strip with plate No. 2 —
Scott No. 2112a
Quantity: 1,000+

Plate strips sell for more than plate pairs. Paste up strips exist spliced with a variety of kinds and colors of cellophane, masking, and paper tapes. Exists miscut.

Flag over Capitol. March 29, 1985. Engraved.

22c red, blue & black

IM 478 imperf pair   20.00
imperf strip with plate No.*   *175.00*
Scott No. 2115a
Quantity: few thousand pairs

*Price for strips of 5 or 6 and price may vary depending on plate number. Plate numbers 1, 3, 5, 7, 10 & 12 have been reported. Exists miscut.

Winter Special Olympics. March 5, 1985. Photogravure.

22c multicolored

IM 479 vrt pair, imperf hz   *900.00*
Scott No. 2142a
Quantity: 80-100 pairs reported

Love. April 17, 1985. Photogravure.

22c multicolored

IM 480 imperf pair   —
Scott No. 2143 var
Quantity: 5 pairs imperf, 5 pairs
partially imperf - see note

Due to the nature of this error, some pairs may contain perfs at left and on top and bottom of the left stamp.

Sea Shells. April 4, 1985. Se-tenant booklet pane of 10. Engraved.

22c multicolored

    a) Frilled Dogwinkle
    b) Reticulated Helmet
    c) New England Neptune
    d) Calico Scallop
    e) Lightning Whelk

IM 481 booklet pane of 10, imperf vrt
between   —
Scott No. 2121a var
Quantity: n/a

Abigail Adams. June 14, 1985. Photogravure.

22c multicolored.

IM 482 imperf pair   *450.00*
Scott No. 2146a
Quantity: 150-200 pairs

Christmas Poinsettia. October 31, 1985. Photogravure.

22c multicolored

IM 483	imperf pair	*175.00*
	block of 4, imperf	—
	plate block of 4, imperf	—
	Zip block of 4, imperf	—
	Scott No. 2166a	
	Quantity: 250-300 pairs	

Christmas Madonna. October 31, 1985. Photogravure.

22c multicolored

IM 484	imperf pair	*175.00*
	Scott No. 2165a	
	Quantity: 250-300 pairs	

COIL STAMP

George Washington. November 6, 1985. Photogravure.

18c multicolored

IM 485	imperf pair, precancelled USA	
	PRESORTED FIRST-CLASS	*375.00*
	Scott No. 2149c	
	Quantity: 50 pairs reported	

IM 486	imperf pair, without precancel	—
	Scott No. 2149b	
	Quantity: *new, 20 pairs reported*	

Arkansas Statehood. January 3, 1986. Photogravure.

22c multicolored

IM 487	vrt pair, imperf hz	—
	Scott No. 2167 var	
	Quantity: 50 pairs reported	

Texas Sesquicentennial. March 2, 1986. Photogravure.

22c multicolored

IM 488	hz pair, imperf vrt	—
	Scott No. 2204a	
	Quantity: 50 pairs	

Public Hospitals. April 11, 1986. Photogravure.

22c multicolored

IM 489	vrt pair, imperf hz	—
	Scott No. 2210a	
	Quantity: 50-75 pairs	

Duke Ellington. April 29, 1986. Photogravure.

22c multicolored

IM 490 vrt pair, imperf hz   —
Scott No. 2211a
Quantity: 50-60 pairs

Wood Carving. October 1, 1986. Se-tenant blocks of 4. Photogravure.

22c multicolored
a) Nautical Figure
b) Cigar Store Indian
c) Highlander Figure
d) Ship Figurehead

IM 491 block of 4 (a-d), imperf vrt   —
Scott No. 2243 var
Quantity: 10 blocks of 4
reported

Buying or Selling?
Consult the dealer directory at the back of the catalogue.

AIR MAIL STAMPS

Beacon on Sherman Hill. July 25, 1928. Engraved.

5c red & blue

IMA 1 vrt pair, imperf between vrt
strip of 3, imperf between LRS (81)   *7,150.00*
Scott No. C11a
Quantity: very rare

Winged Globe. February 10, 1930. Engraved. Flat plate press.

5c violet

IMA 2 hz pair, imperf between   —
bottom strip of 5 with plate
No., left pair imperf between
LRS (86)   *3960.00*
Scott No. C12a
Quantity: very rare

Eagle & Shield. May 14, 1938. Engraved.

6c red & blue

IMA 3 vrt pair, imperf hz   375.00
as above, line pair   —
as above, used on cover
postmarked 5/15/38   *300.00*
plate block of 4, imperf hz   *750.00*
Scott No. C23a
Quantity: few thousand pairs

IMA 4 hz pair, imperf vrt LRS (86)   *6,600.00*
Scott No. C23b
Quantity: 5 pairs

Transport Plane. June 25, 1941. Engraved.

6c carmine red

IMA 5 hz pair, imperf between   2,000.00
Scott No. C25b
Quantity: 20 pairs

Government crayon marks are usually present on this error.

Statue of Liberty at New York. August 30, 1947. Engraved.

15c green

IMA 6 hz pair, imperf between   1,900.00
Scott No. C35a
Quantity: 20 pairs

Statue of Liberty. June 28, 1961. Engraved & lithographed.

15c orange & black

IMA 7	hz pair, imperf vrt LRS (79)	*11,500.00*
	strip of 5, 3 stamps & margin at left imperf vrt LRS (86)	*9,075.00*
	strip of 5, 3 stamps at left imperf vrt LRS (81)	*15,400.00*
	Scott No. 63b	
	Quantity: 3 as listed above	

COIL STAMPS

Runway of Stars. January 5, 1968. Engraved.

10c red

IMA 8	imperf pair	450.00
	line pair, imperf	750.00
	paste up pair, imperf	—
	Scott No. C73a	
	Quantity: 100+ pairs	

Jet Aircraft. May 7, 1971. Engraved

11c red

IMA 9	imperf pair	200.00
	line pair, imperf	350.00
	Scott No. C82a	
	Quantity: fewer than 200 pairs reported	

Exists miscut. Slightly miscut pairs usually sell for less than listed pairs; dramatically miscut pairs often sell for more than listed pairs.

Envelope with Wings. December 27, 1973. Engraved.

13c red

IMA 10	imperf pair	100.00
	line pair, imperf	150.00
	Scott No. C83a	
	Quantity: 500+ pairs	

Phillip Mazzei. October 13, 1980. Photogravure.

40c multicolored

IMA 11	imperf pair	*2,500.00*
	Scott No. C98b	
	Quantity: 15 pairs reported	

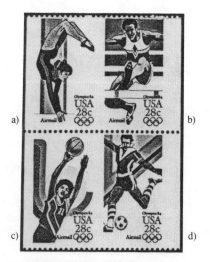

Olympics. June 17, 1983. Photogravure.

28c multicolored

a) Gymnastics
b) Hurdles
c) Basketball
d) Soccer

IMA 12 block of 4 (a-d), imperf vrt
LRS(86)   *3,400.00*
as above, plate block of 4   —
Scott No. C101-104 var
Quantity: the 2 blocks as listed

a) ... b) ... c) ... d)

Olympics. April 8, 1983. Photogravure.

40c multicolored

a) *Shot Put*
b) *Gymnastics*
c) *Swimming*
d) *Weight Lifting*

IMA 13 block of 4 (a-d), imperf   *1,500.00*
copyright block of 4, imperf   —
vrt pair (a & c) or (b & d),
imperf   —
Scott No. C108b
Quantity: 30-40 blocks of 4,
20-30 pairs reported

Where possible, illustrations of actual error stamps were used. They are bordered in black. Where photos of errors were unavailable, illustrations of normal stamps were used. They appear without any border.

Alfred V. Verville. February 13, 1985. Photogravure.

33c multicolored

IMA 14 imperf pair   *1,100.00*
plate block of 4, imperf   —
Scott No. C113a
Quantity: 50-75 pairs reported

Lawrence & Elmer Sperry. February 13, 1985. Photogravure.

39c multicolored

IMA 15 imperf pair   *1,000.00*
Scott No. C114a
Quantity: 25 pairs reported

Many are faulty.

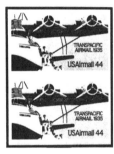

Transpacific Airmail 1935. February 15, 1985. Photogravure.

44c multicolored

IMA 16 imperf pair   *1,100.00*
Scott No. C115 var
Quantity: 25 pairs reported

Junipero Serra. August 22, 1985. Photogravure.

44c multicolored

IMA 17 imperf pair   —
Scott No. 116a
Quantity: *19 pairs reported*

SPECIAL DELIVERY

Messenger & Tablet. October 10, 1894. Engraved.

10c blue

IMSD 1 hz pair, imperf   —
vertical block of 6, without
gum, imperf LRS (86)   *8,800.00*
Scott No. E4a
Quantity: very rare

**Messenger & Tablet. October 16, 1895. Engraved.
Double line watermark.**

10c blue

IMSD 2 imperf pair   *3,000.00*
sheet margin single, imperf   —
Scott No. E5a
Quantity: very rare

**Motorcycle Messenger. November 29, 1927.
Engraved.**

10c violet

IMSD 3 hz pair, imperf between   200.00
plate block of 4, imperf vrt
between   —
Scott No. E15c
Quantity: n/a

**Great Seal of the United States. February 10, 1936.
Engraved.**

16c red & blue

IMSD 4 hz pair, imperf vrt   *2,500.00*
Scott No. CE2a
Quantity: 10 pairs reported

POSTAGE DUE

SERIES OF 1879

Printed by the American Bank Note Company.

Numeral. September 18, 1879. Engraved.

10c light brown

IMPD 1 imperf pair   *1,650.00*
Scott No. J5a
Quantity: rare

SERIES OF 1891

Printed by the American Bank Note Company.

Numeral. 1891. Engraved.
1c bright claret

IMPD 2 imperf pair **NRI**   *300.00*
Scott No. J22a
Quantity: 46 stamps

See note for Issues of the American Bank Note Company, 1890/1893.

Numeral. 1891. Engraved.
2c bright claret

IMPD 3 imperf pair   *300.00*
Scott No. J23a
Quantity: 46 stamps

Numeral. 1891. Engraved.

   3c bright claret

IMPD 4 imperf pair   *300.00*
         Scott No. J24a
         Quantity: 46 stamps

Numeral. 1891. Engraved.

   5c bright claret

IMPD 5 imperf pair   *300.00*
         Scott No. J25a
         Quantity: 46 stamps

Numeral. 1891. Engraved.

   10c bright claret

IMPD 6 imperf pair   *300.00*
          Scott No. J26a
         Quantity: 46 stamps

Numeral. 1891. Engraved.

   30c bright claret

IMPD 7 imperf pair   *300.00*
          Scott No. J27a
         Quantity: 46 stamps

Numeral. 1891. Engraved.

   50c bright claret

IMPD 8 imperf pair   *300.00*
          Scott No. J28a
         Quantity: 46 stamps

Numeral. August 14, 1894. Engraved.

   1c deep claret

IMPD 9 imperf pair   *250.00*
         block of 4, imperf   —
         Scott No. J31a
         Quantity: n/a

        Usually encountered without gum. Price is for copy without gum.

IMPD 10 vrt pair, imperf hz   —
         Scott No. J31b
         Quantity: n/a

OFFICIAL STAMPS

Post Office Department. Numeral. 1873. Engraved.

   15c black

IMO 1 imperf pair   *750.00*
         Scott No. O53a
         Quantity: rare

War Department. George Washington. 1879. Engraved.

3c rose red

IMO 2   imperf pair   *900.00*
Scott No. O116a
Quantity: rare

COIL STAMP

Official Mail. January 12, 1983. Engraved.

20c black, red & blue

IMO 3   imperf pair   *850.00*
Scott No. O135a
Quantity: fewer than 25 pairs
reported

MIGRATORY BIRD HUNTING STAMPS

Mallards. July 1934. Engraved.

$1 blue

IMWF 1 imperf pair   **PW**   *2,500.00*
vrt strip of 3, imperf LRS (85)   *3,850.00*
Scott No. RW1a
Quantity: very rare

Most copies of this error exist without gum and with faults and copies have been reported with revenue stamps printed on the reverse.

IMWF 2 vrt pair, imperf hz   **PW**   —
Scott No. RW1b
Quantity: very rare

IMWF 2 is known to exist with gum on the front of the stamp. Some experts believe that it is possible that copies of IMWF 1 have been created by trimming the perforations off and removing the gum from the front of IMWF 2.

COLOR OMITTED ERRORS

Red Cross. May 21, 1931. Engraved.

2c black & red

CO 1 red omitted —
Scott No. 702 var
Quantity: unique

This error results from a paper fold between the black design and the application of the red cross. It is contained in a multiple at lower left.

American Music. October 15, 1964. Engraved.

5c red, blue & black (gray paper)

CO 2 blue omitted *1,250.00*
Scott No. 1252a
Quantity: 20-40 reported

☞ Caution. Should contain no traces of blue. Copies with traces of blue are do not qualify as errors.

Florida Settlement. August 28, 1965. Engraved.

5c red, black & ocher
CO 3 ocher omitted 600.00
Scott No. 1271a
Quantity: 300-400

Marine Corps Reserve. August 29, 1966. Engraved, lithographed.

5c black and ocher (engraved); red & blue (lithographed)

CO 4 black & ocher omitted LRS (86) *8,800.00*
Scott No. 1315b
Quantity: unique

Where possible, illustrations of actual error stamps were used. They are bordered in black. Where photos of errors were unavailable, illustrations of normal stamps were used. They appear without any border.

Savings Bonds. October 26, 1966. Engraved, lithographed.

5c red, black, dark blue (engraved); light blue (lithographed)

CO 5 red, black & dark blue (engraved) omitted *3,500.00*
Scott No. 1320b
Quantity: 6 reported

Davy Crockett. August 17, 1967. Engraved, lithographed.

5c black & gray green (engraved);
yellow & green (lithographed)

CO 6   gray green (engraved) omitted   —
Scott No. 1330 var
Quantity: unique

CO 7   black & gray green (engraved) omitted   —
Scott No. 1330 var
Quantity: unique

CO 8   yellow & green (litho) omitted   —
Scott No. 1330 var
Quantity: unique

Space Capsule. September 29, 1967. Engraved, lithographed.

5c dark blue & blue green (engraved);
red & light blue (lithographed)

CO 9   red omitted   125.00
block of 9, red omitted on center stamp   175.00
Scott No. 1332 var
Quantity: 500

Hemisfair '68. March 30, 1968. Engraved, lithographed.

6c white (engraved); red &
Prussian blue (lithographed)

CO 10   white omitted   *1,350.00*
Scott No. 1340a
Quantity: 100

Walt Disney. September 11, 1968. Photogravure.

6c multicolored

CO 11   black omitted   2,000.00
as above, plate block of 4   —
Scott No. 1355d
Quantity: 35 reported

CO 12   blue omitted   1,750.00
as above, plate block of 4   —
Scott No. 1355f
Quantity: 35 reported

CO 13   ocher omitted   800.00
as above, plate block of 4   —
Scott No. 1355a
Quantity: 400-500

Waterfowl Conservation. October 24, 1968. Engraved, lithographed.

> 6c black (engraved); red, blue, blue green
> & yellow (lithographed)

CO 14   red & blue omitted   1,750.00
as above, plate block of 4 LRS (86)   *5,060.00*
used   *600.00*
Scott No. 1362b
Quantity: 50

Christmas Angel. November 1, 1968. Engraved, lithographed.

> 6c red, brown, blue & black (engraved);
> yellow (lithographed)

CO 15   yellow omitted   150.00
as above, plate block of 10   —
Scott No. 1363c
Quantity: 1,000+

Grandma Moses. May 1, 1969. Engraved, lithographed.

> 6c black & Prussian blue (engraved); red,
> yellow, blue & blue green (lithographed)

CO 16   black & Prussian blue omitted   1,000.00
as above, plate block of 4   —
Scott No. 1370b
Quantity: 150

Usually encountered with mottled gum. Price is for copy with mottled gum.

Professional Baseball. September 24, 1969. Engraved, lithographed.

> 6c black (engraved); red,
> green & yellow (lithographed)

CO 17   black omitted   1,000.00
Scott No. 1381a
Quantity: 100-150

Exists with tagging ghosts.

Christmas. November 3, 1969. Engraved.

> 6c dark green & dark brown (engraved);
> red, yellow & light green (lithographed)

CO 18   yellow omitted   —
Scott No 1384e
Quantity: very rare

CO 19   light green omitted   45.00
Scott No. 1384c
Quantity: 1,000+

CO 20   yellow, light green & red omitted   1,200.00
as above, used   *750.00*
Scott No. 1384d
Quantity: 50-60 unused, 6 copies
used reported

Christmas Nativity Scene. November 5, 1970. Photogravure.

6c multicolored

CO 21   black omitted   *1,100.00*
Scott No. 1414b
Quantity: 50

☛ Caution. Many copies similar to the error exist with partial black. However, in order to qualify as an error no trace of black should be visible under 30 power magnification. Expert certificate recommended.

Christmas Precancel. November 5, 1970. Photogravure.

6c multicolored, precancelled with black bars

CO 22   blue omitted   1,400.00
strip of 3, blue omitted on 1 stamp, partial color on 1 stamp, and complete color on 1 stamp   1,400.00
Scott No. 1414c
Quantity: 15 reported

Often occurs in strips with some stamps in the strip having blue color.

a)   b)

c)   d)

Christmas Toys. November 5, 1970. Se-tenant block of 4. Photogravure by Guilford Gravure, Inc.

6c multicolored

     a) Doll carriage
     b) Toy Horse
     c) Tricycle
     d) Locomotive

CO 23   block of 4, black omitted   —
any single, black omitted   *2,000.00*
Scott No. 1418d
Quantity: 2 blocks, 5-6 of each single reported

Landing of Pilgrims. November 21, 1970. Engraved, lithographed.

6c black (engraved); red, yellow & blue (lithographed)

CO 24   yellow omitted   1,250.00
Scott No. 1420a
Quantity: 200

a)   b)

c)   d)

Wildlife Conservation. June 12, 1971. Se-tenant blocks of 4. Engraved, lithographed.

8c dark brown, dark green & black (engraved); red, blue, buff, olive green & bluish green (lithographed)

     a) Trout
     b) Alligator
     c) Polar Bear
     d) California Condor

CO 25 block of 4, olive & bluish green
omitted from a & b   *3,000.00*
as above, plate block of 4   —
Scott No. 1430b
Quantity: 8 blocks including unique
plate block

CO 26 block of 4, red omitted from a, c & d   —
used single (a), red omitted   *500.00*
Scott No 1430c
Quantity: very rare

Due to color schemes used in the four designs, some colors are normally not present in every stamp. For example, lithographic red was not used in the alligator design and, therefore, cannot be considered to have been omitted.

☞ Caution. The red head of the condor can appear to be omitted if shifted to the lower left. Certificate of authenticity advised.

American Revolution Bicentennial. July 4, 1971. Engraved, lithographed.

8c gray & black (engraved); red & blue (lithographed)

CO 27 black & gray omitted   950.00
Scott No. 1432a
Quantity: 100-150

CO 28 gray omitted   *1,000.00*
Scott No. 1432b
Quantity: n/a

CO 28 often occurs in pairs or larger multiples with gray completely omitted from one stamp and gray and black partially omitted from others.

Space Achievement. August 2, 1971. Se-tenant pairs. Engraved, lithographed.

8c black (engraved); red, yellow, blue & gray (lithographed)
    a) Earth & Sun
    b) Lunar Vehicle

CO 29 pair, red & blue omitted   *1,450.00*
single b, red & blue omitted   *750.00*
Scott No. 1434b
Quantity: 40 pairs, 10 singles
reported

☞ Caution. The flag on the lunar lander is often shifted into the lander and not visible.

    CO 30   **CO 31**

Emily Dickinson. August 28, 1971. Engraved, lithographed.

8c black & light olive green (engraved); dark olive green, red & flesh tone (lithographed); (greenish paper)

CO 30 black & light olive green omitted   900.00
as above, plate block of 4   —
Scott No. 1436a
Quantity: 150

CO 31 pair, flesh tone omitted on one
stamp   *10,000.00*
Scott No. 1436b
Quantity: 2-3

a)    b)

c)    **Normal Block**   d)

Historic Preservation. October 29, 1971. Setenant blocks of 4. Engraved, lithographed.

8c black brown (engraved); beige (lithographed); (buff paper)
    a) Decauter Home
    b) The Charles W. Morgan
    c) Cable Car
    d) San Xavier Mission

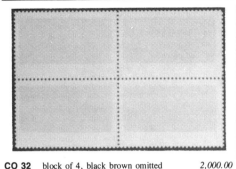

CO 32 block of 4, black brown omitted   *2,000.00*
Scott No. 1443b
Quantity: 16 blocks of 4 reported

CO 33 block of 4, beige omitted   *3,750.00*
Scott No. 1443c
Quantity: 8 blocks of 4

Two blocks of CO 33 are damaged and one is reportedly broken.

Christmas. November 10, 1971. Photogravure.

8c multicolored

CO 34 gold omitted   550.00
as above, plate block   —
Scott No. 1444a
Quantity: 150-200

a)   b)

c)   d)

National Parks Centennial. April 5, 1972. Setenant blocks of 4. Engraved, lithographed.

2c black & dark blue (engraved); red,
yellow, blue, tan & black (lithographed)
  a) Wrecked Hull
  b) Lighthouse
  c) Shorebirds
  d) Shorebirds & Grass

CO 36 block of 4, black (litho) omitted   *1,850.00*
Scott No. 1451b
Quantity: 25 blocks of 4 reported

a)   b)

c)   d)

Wildlife Conservation. September 20, 1972. Setenant blocks of 4. Engraved, lithographed.

8c black (engraved); red, yellow, blue,
green, brown & beige (lithographed)
  a) Fur Seal
  b) Cardinal
  c) Brown Pelican
  d) Bighorn Sheep

CO 37 block of 4, brown omitted   *2,500.00*
as above, plate block of 4   *3,000.00*
single (c or d), brown omitted   *600.00*
Scott No. 1467b
Quantity: 8-16 blocks of 4 reported

CO 38 block of 4, blue & green omitted   *3,500.00*
as above, plate block of 4   *4,000.00*
Scott No. 1464-7c
Quantity: 8 blocks of 4 reported

CO 39   **CO 40**

Tom Sawyer. October 13, 1972. Engraved, lithographed.

8c black & deep red (engraved); red,
blue, yellow & gray (lithographed)

CO 39 engraved black & red omitted   *1,100.00*
as above, plate block of 4 (plate
No. also omitted)   —
Scott No. 1470b
Quantity: 150

CO 40 red, blue, yellow & gray omitted *1,450.00*
Scott No. 1470c
Quantity: 50

Christmas Angels. November 9, 1972. Photogravure.

8c multicolored
CO 41 pair, black omitted on right stamp *2,350.00*
Scott No. 1471b
Quantity: 10 pairs reported

CO 42 pink omitted 450.00
as above, plate block of 12 —
Scott No. 1471a
Quantity: few hundred

Pharmacy. November 10, 1972. Engraved, lithographed.

8c black (engraved); orange, yellow, blue
& purplish red (lithographed)
CO 44 orange & blue omitted *1,100.00*
as above, plate block of 4 —
Scott No. 1473a
Quantity: 150 reported

CO 45 blue omitted —
Scott No.: 1473b
Quantity: 2-3

Stamp Collecting. November 17, 1972. Engraved, lithographed.

8c brown & black (engraved); greenish
blue & black (lithographed)

CO 46 black (litho) omitted 1,000.00
as above, plate block of 4 —
Scott No. 1474a
Quantity: 80-100

The lithographed part of the design consists of a pattern of dots printed on the greenish blue field. They are visible under magnification on the normal stamp.

a)

b)

c)

d)

Boston Tea Party. July 4, 1973. Se-tenant blocks of 4. Engraved, lithographed.

8c black (engraved); red, yellow, blue &
black (lithographed)
a) Tea Cast Overboard
b) Ship
c) Boat & Keel
d) Pier

CO 47 block of 4, black (engraved) omitted 2,300.00
hz pair (a & c) or (b & d) black
(engraved) omitted —
Scott No. 1483b
Quantity: 80 blocks of 4 reported
including one without gum; sets of
horizontal pairs also exist

CO 48 block or 4, black (litho) omitted *1,750.00*
as above, Zip block —
Scott No. 1483c
Quantity: 32 blocks 4

CO 49   CO 50

Copernicus. April 23, 1973. Engraved, lithographed.

8c black (engraved); yellow (lithographed)

CO 49   yellow omitted   1,250.00
        as above, plate block of 4   —
        as above, Zip block of 4   —
        Scott No. 1488a
        Quantity: 100

☛ Caution. Dangerous fakes exist. Known copies of this error each have an APS certificate. Copies without certificates should be regarded with extreme suspicion.

CO 50   black omitted   1,500.00
        Scott No. 1488b
        Quantity: 100

Progress in Electronics. July 10, 1973. Engraved, lithographed.

8c black (engraved); orange, dark brown, tan, green & light violet (lithographed)

CO 51   tan & light violet omitted   *1,700.00*
        Scott No. 1501b
        Quantity: 50

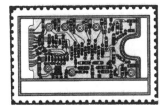

CO 52   black omitted   800.00
        Scott No. 1501a
        Quantity: 300-400

Progress in Electronics. July 10, 1973. Engraved, lithographed.

15c black (engraved); yellow, brown, gray & gray green (lithographed)

CO 53   black omitted   1,750.00
        Scott No. 1502a
        Quantity: 50

Rural America. October 5, 1973. Engraved, lithographed.

8c black, dark blue & brown red (engraved); yellow, green, orange brown & brown (lithographed)

CO 54   green & orange brown omitted   625.00
        Scott No. 1504a
        Quantity: 100

Rural America. August 16, 1974. Engraved, lithographed.

10c black & dark blue (engraved); red, yellow, gray blue & brown (lithographed)

CO 55   black & dark blue omitted   650.00
        Scott No. 1506a
        Quantity: 100

Crossed Flags. December 8, 1973. Engraved.

10c red & blue

CO 56 blue omitted   200.00
pair, one normal & one with blue
omitted   250.00
single, blue omitted, used on cover   *250.00*
Scott No. 1509b
Quantity: 100-125 singles or pairs
with one normal attached; 2-3 used

Zip Code. January 24, 1974. Photogravure.

10c multicolored

CO 57 yellow omitted   60.00
as above, plate block of 8   *500.00*
Scott No. 1511a
Quantity: 1,000+

☛ Caution. Dangerous fakes exist.

Horse Racing. May 4, 1974. Photogravure.

10c multicolored

CO 58 blue omitted   *1,500.00*
Scott No 1528a
Quantity: 50-100

CO 59 red omitted   —
Scott No 1528b
Quantity: 1-4 reported

☛ Caution. In order to qualify as the error all traces of red must be absent under 30 power magnification. Many copies containing traces of red are offered as the error, therefore, caution is advised.

a)   b)

c)   d)

Mineral Heritage. June 13, 1974. Se-tenant blocks of 4. Engraved, lithographed.

10c black, red, violet (engraved); light blue, gray, yellow, brown & green (lithographed)

a) *Amethyst*
b) *Rhodochrosite*
c) *Tourmaline*
d) *Petrified Wood*

CO 60 block of 4, light blue omitted (a-d),
yellow omitted (a & d)   *2,000.00*
single a or d, yellow & lt blue
omitted   —
single b or c, light blue omitted   —
Scott No. listed variously as 1538a,
1539a, 1540a & 1541b-c
Quantity: 24 blocks of 4

Light blue (the lithographed background color) was printed on all four stamps. Lithographic yellow was normally printed only on stamps a and d, therefore its absence on those stamps is not the result of an error.

☛ Caution. Dangerous fakes exist.

CO 61 single b, red & black (engraved)
omitted   —
Scott No. 1541d
Quantity: 4 reported

CO 62 single c, violet & black (engraved)
omitted   —
Scott No. 1539b
Quantity: 4

The error stamps CO 61 & CO 62 result from a single sheet in which one se-tenant row, containing the two designs, lacked the engraved colors, black (inscription) and red or violet (mineral color) respectively.

Normal Stamp   Error Stamp

Kentucky Settlement. June 15, 1974. Engraved, lithographed.

10c black & dark green (engraved); light green, blue, black, tan and light red (lithographed)

CO 63 black & dark green (engraved), black, green & blue (litho) omitted   *2,500.00*
Scott No. 1542b
Quantity: 29 reported including those in strips of 3 or 10

Exists in strips of 3 containing one normal, one with colors partially omitted and one with listed colors completely omitted. Also exists in strips of 10 (with various stages of colors omitted) which tend to bring substantial premiums.

CO 64 black (litho) omitted   1,100.00
as above, plate block of 4   —
used single, black omitted   —
Scott No. 1542a
Quantity: 100-150

CO 65

CO 66

Energy Conservation. September 23, 1974. Engraved, lithographed.

10c black (engraved); purple, blue, orange, yellow & green (lithographed).

CO 65 blue & orange omitted   *600.00*
Scott No. 1547a
Quantity: 100-200

CO 66 orange & green omitted   *500.00*
Scott No. 1547b
Quantity: 100-200

CO 67 green omitted   *700.00*
Scott No. 1547c
Quantity: 100-200

Christmas. October 23, 1974. Photogravure.

10c black, blue, yellow, magenta & very light buff   —

CO 68 buff omitted
Scott No. 1551 var
Quantity: 1,500 reported

☛ Caution. The buff color is a very light, transparent shade. Errors are extremely difficult to distinguish from normal stamps. Certificate of authenticity is strongly recommended.

Pioneer - Jupiter. February 28, 1975. Engraved, lithographed.

10c dark blue (engraved); yellow & red (lithographed)

CO 69 dark blue omitted   *1,050.00*
Scott No. 1556b
Quantity: 200 reported

Where possible, illustrations of actual error stamps were used. They are bordered in black. Where photos of errors were unavailable, illustrations of normal stamps were used. They appear without any border.

CO 70 red & yellow omitted *1,300.00*
Zip block of 4 —
Scott No. 1556a
Quantity: 50-100 reported

Mariner 10. April 4, 1975. Engraved, lithographed.

10c black (engraved); red, brown & blue (lithographed)

CO 71 red omitted 400.00
as above, plate block of 4 —
Scott No. 1557a
Quantity: 300-400

☛ Caution. The red star may be shifted down and hidden in the spacecraft giving the appearance of being the error stamp. Examine carefully.

CO 72 brown & blue omitted *1,750.00*
Scott No. 1557b
Quantity: 50

YOUTHFUL HEROINE
On the dark night of April 26, 1777, 16-year-old Sybil Ludington rode her horse "Star" alone through the Connecticut countryside rallying her father's militia to repel a raid by the British on Danbury.

Reverse Inscription

Sybil Ludington. March 25, 1975. Photogravure.

8c multicolored, green inscription on reverse

CO 73 green reverse inscription omitted 375.00
Scott No. 1559a
Quantity: *50-100*

☛ Caution. Green reverse inscriptions are printed in a partially water soluble ink, therefore, used copies without certificates of authenticity should be regarded with suspicion.

GALLANT SOLDIER
The conspicuously courageous actions of black foot soldier Salem Poor at the Battle of Bunker Hill on June 17, 1775, earned him citations for his bravery and leadership ability.

Reverse Inscription

Salem Poor. March 25, 1975. Photogravure.

10c multicolored, green inscription on reverse

CO 74 green reverse inscription omitted 350.00
Scott No. 1560a
Quantity: 300+ reported

☛ Caution. Green reverse inscriptions are printed in a partially water soluble ink, therefore, used copies without certificates of authenticity should be regarded with suspicion.

Haym Salomon. March 25, 1975. Photogravure.

10c multicolored, green inscription on reverse

CO 75 red omitted *300.00*
Scott No. 1561b
Quantity: *50-100*

☛ Caution. Expert certificate recommended.

FINANCIAL HERO
Businessman and broker Haym Salomon was responsible for raising most of the money needed to finance the American Revolution and later to save the new nation from collapse.

Reverse Inscription

CO 76 green reverse inscription
omitted 350.00
as above, used single 70.00
Scott No. 1561a
Quantity: 200-300

☛ Caution. Green reverse inscriptions are printed in a partially water soluble ink, therefore, used copies without certificates of authenticity should be regarded with suspicion.

D. W. Griffith. May 27, 1975. Engraved, lithographed.

10c dark brown (engraved);
violet, blue, yellow, &
magenta (lithographed)

CO 77 dark brown omitted *750.00*
Scott No. 1555a
Quantity: 50-100

a)   b)

c)   d)

200 Years of Postal Service. September 3, 1975. Se-tenant blocks of 4. Photogravure.

10 multicolored

a) Locomotive
b) Stagecoach
c) Satellite
d) Biplane

CO 78 block of 4, red (10c denomina-tion) omitted *5,000.00*
Scott No. 1575b
Quantity: 3-4 block of 4 reported

Two plates for red were used; one for the denomination and another for other design elements. Only the red denomination is omitted and red printed from the second plate appears elsewhere in on the stamp.

a)   b)

Banking & Commerce. October 6, 1975. Se-tenant pairs. Engraved, lithographed.

10c dark brown, green,
greenish gray (engraved);
yellow, blue & brown (lithographed)

a) Banking
b) Commerce

CO 79 pair, blue & brown omitted *950.00*
single a or b, blue & brown omitted —
Scott No. 1577b
Quantity: 32-48 pairs; 16-24 singles

AMERICANA SERIES OF 1975/1981

Eagle with Shield. December 1, 1975. Photogravure.

13c multicolored

CO 80 yellow omitted 200.00
Scott No. 1596b
Quantity: 300-500

☛ Caution. Many changlings exist. Certificate of authenticity strongly recommended.

Flag. June 30, 1978. Engraved.

15c red, blue & gray

CO 81 gray omitted *125.00*
Scott No. 1597b
Quantity: 100-200

Stamps with gray partially omitted exist.

Lamp. September 11, 1979. Engraved, lithographed.

50c black (engraved); orange & tan
(lithographed)

CO 82 black omitted *500.00*
Scott No.: 1608 var
Quantity: 120-150 reported

Exists in strips with some stamps showing partial omission of black. Strips sell for premiums.

Candle Holder. July 2, 1979. Engraved, lithographed.

$1 dark brown (engraved); yellow, orange & tan (lithographed)

CO 83 dark brown omitted   *450.00*
as above, plate block of 4   —
Scott No. 1610a
Quantity: 800+

Can be found in combination with normal stamps. Tagging ghosts exist.

CO 84 yellow, orange & tan omitted   *400.00*
Scott No. 1610b
Quantity: 600-800

COIL STAMP

Flag. June 30, 1978. Engraved.

15c red, blue & gray

CO 85 gray omitted   *60.00*
Scott No. 1618Cf
Quantity: 1,000+

Most show bleed of blue into area of gray.

BICENTENNIAL SOUVENIR SHEETS

A great variety of colors omitted and imperforate varieties exist, many with multiple errors. Those which are imperforate as well as having colors omitted are listed in the imperforates section of the catalogue. Those normally perforated but lacking one or more colors are listed below.

Surrender at Yorktown. May 29, 1976. Souvenir sheet of 5 stamps. Lithographed.

13c multicolored

CO 86 yellow (USA 13c) omitted on 1st &
5th stamps   —
as above, used, 5/29/76 Philadelphia, PA first day cancellation   —
Scott No. 1686g
Quantity: very rare

CO 87 yellow (USA 13c) omitted on 5th
stamp   —
Scott No. 1686l
Quantity: very rare

CO 88 brown (USA 13c) omitted on 2nd
stamp, orange (USA 13c) omitted
on 3rd & 4th stamps LRS (85)   1,430.00
Scott No. 1686i
Quantity: very rare

CO 89 orange (USA 13c) omitted on 3rd &
4th stamps   —
Scott No. 1686k
Quantity: very rare

For imperforate varieties of Bicentennial souvenir sheets with color(s) omitted refer to the imperforate section of the catalogue.

The Declaration of Independence. May 29, 1976. Souvenir sheet of 5 stamps. Lithographed.

18c multicolored

CO 94   brown (USA 18c) omitted on 1st & 3rd stamps
Scott No. 1687g
Quantity: 5-10   —

CO 95   orange (USA 18c) omitted on 2nd & 5th stamps, yellow (USA 18c) omitted on 4th stamp
Scott No. 1687h
Quantity: very rare   —

CO 96   orange (USA 18c) omitted on 2nd & 5th stamps
Scott No. 1687m
Quantity: very rare   —

CO 97   yellow (USA 18c) omitted on 4th stamp
Scott No. 1687i
Quantity: very rare   —

CO 98   black (screened dots for contrast in mural) omitted
Scott No. 1687j
Quantity: very rare   —

CO 99   all process colors omitted, sheet blank except for USA 18c, tagging & perfs
Scott No. 1687f
Quantity: unique   —

The term "process colors" refers to those colors which were reduced to a pattern of dots and printed atop one another to achieve the effect of full color. The denominations and "USA" were added by a separate operation and printed in "solid color" rather than in a pattern of dots. The difference in printing can be seen on a normal sheet by examination under 10 power magnification.

Washington Crossing the Delaware. May 29, 1976. Souvenir sheet of 5 stamps. Lithographed.

24c multicolored

CO 104   blue (USA 24c) omitted on 1st stamp, light blue (USA 24c) omitted on 2nd & 3rd stamps
Scott No. 1688i
Quantity: very rare   —

CO 105   blue (USA 24c) omitted on 1st stamp, light blue (USA 24c) omitted on 2nd & 3rd stamps, with 5/29/76 Philadelphia, PA first day cancellation
Scott No. 1688i
Quantity: very rare   —

CO 106   white (USA 24c) omitted on 4th & 5th stamps
Scott No. 1688g
Quantity: very rare   —

CO 107   white (USA 24c) omitted on 4th & 5th stamps with 5/29/76 Philadelphia, PA first day cancellation, perforations inverted
Scott No. 1688g
Quantity: very rare   —

CO 108   all process colors omitted, sheet blank except for USA 24c, tagging & perfs
Scott No. 1688h
Quantity: unique   —

See note after CO 99.

Washington at Valley Forge. May 29, 1976. Souvenir sheet of 5 stamps. Lithographed.

31c multicolored

CO 110 gray (USA 31c) omitted on 1st & 3rd stamps   —
Scott No. 1689g
Quantity: very rare

CO 111 gray (USA 31c) omitted on 1st & 3rd stamps, white (USA 31c) omitted on 5th stamp   —
Scott No. 1689m
Quantity: very rare

CO 112 brown (USA 31c) omitted on 2nd & 4th stamps   —
Scott No. 1689l
Quantity: very rare

CO 113 brown (USA 31c) omitted on 2nd & 4th stamps, white omitted on 5th stamp   —
Scott No. 1689h
Quantity: very rare

CO 114 white (USA 31c) omitted on 5th stamp   —
Scott No. 1689i
Quantity: rare

CO 115 black (screened process dots in mural) omitted   —
Scott No. 1689j
Quantity: very rare

In process color printing a printed screen of black dots is often used to intensify contrast and add crispness to the finished illustration.

Benjamin Franklin. June 1, 1976. Engraved, lithographed.

13c dark blue (engraved); light blue, brown & yellow (lithographed)

CO 118 light blue omitted   550.00
as above, plate block of 4   —
Scott No. 1690a
Quantity: 600-800 reported

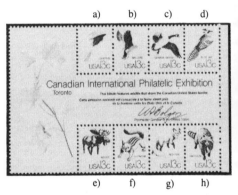

CAPEX. June 10, 1978. Souvenir sheet of 8 stamps. Engraved, lithographed.

13c dark green & black (engraved); yellow, red, blue, brown, light green & black (lithographed)

    a) Cardinal
    b) Mallard
    c) Canada Goose
    d) Blue Jay
    e) Moose
    f) Chipmunk
    g) Red Fox
    h) Raccoon

CO 120 souvenir sheet of 8, all lithographed colors omitted   —
as above, with plate No.   —
Scott No. 1757i
Quantity: 6 souvenir sheets reported

CO 121 single (d or h), engraved black omitted   —
Scott No. 1757 var
Quantity: very rare

Christmas. October 18, 1979. Photogravure.

15c multicolored

CO 123   yellow & green omitted, black
      misaligned   750.00
      Scott No. 1800a
      Quantity: 150

CO 124   yellow, green & tan omitted, black
      misaligned   675.00
      Scott No. 1800b
      Quantity: 250

Ten pairs exist containing one each of CO 123 and CO 124.

General Bernardo Galvez. July 23, 1980. Engraved, lithographed.

15c dark brown, claret & light gray blue
(engraved); red, blue, brown & light
yellow (lithographed)

CO 125   dark brown, claret & light gray blue
      (engraved) omitted   1,250.00
      Scott No. 1826a
      Quantity: 50+

CO 126   red, blue, brown & light yellow
      (litho) omitted   1,250.00
      Scott No. 1826 var
      Quantity: 35-50 reported

Flag over Supreme Court. December 17, 1981. Engraved.

20c black, blue & red

CO 127   black omitted   —
      Scott No. 1894d
      Quantity: n/a

CO 128   blue omitted   185.00
      Scott No. 1894 var
      Quantity: n/a

COIL STAMPS

Flag over Supreme Court. December 17, 1981. Engraved.

20c black, blue & red

CO 129   black omitted   65.00
      strip of 3 with plate No.   —
      Scott No. 1895b
      Quantity: 1,000+

CO 130   blue omitted   —
      Scott No. 1895c
      Quantity: n/a

Edna St. Vincent Millay. July 10, 1981. Engraved, lithographed.

18c black (engraved); yellow, magenta, blue, gray & buff (lithographed)

CO 132   black (engraved) omitted   500.00
     as above, plate block of 4   —
     as above, Zip block of 4   —
     used, black omitted   —
     Scott No. 1926a
     Quantity: 300+

Frederic Remington. October 9, 1981. Engraved, lithographed.

18c dark brown (engraved); light brown, gray green (lithographed)

CO 133   dark brown (engraved) omitted   750.00
     as above, plate block of 4   —
     Scott No. 1934b
     Quantity: 300-400

a)   b)

Yorktown - Virginia Capes. October 16, 1981. Se-tenant pairs. Engraved, lithographed.

18c black (engraved); red, light blue, dark blue, brown & tan (lithographed)
    a) Yorktown
    b) Virginia Capes

CO 134   pair, black (engraved) omitted   775.00
     as above, plate block of 4   —
     single a or b, black (engraved)
     omitted   —
     Scott No. 1938b
     Quantity: 80 pairs, 10 of each
     single reported

LOVE. February 1, 1982. Photogravure.

20c multicolored

CO 135   blue omitted   350.00
     Scott No. 1951c
     Quantity: 100-150

Copies from one sheet of 50 are centered high, with the design running slightly off at the top.

International Peace Garden. June 30, 1982. Engraved, lithographed.

20c black, dark brown & dark green (engraved); red, yellow, green & gray (lithographed)

CO 136   black, dark brown & dark green
     (engraved) omitted   675.00
     Scott No. 2014a
     Quantity: 100-150

Science & Industry. January 19, 1983. Engraved, lithographed.

20c black (engraved); blue, yellow & magenta (lithographed)

CO 137 black (engraved) omitted —
Scott No. 2031a
Quantity: 30-40 reported

Medal of Honor. June 7, 1983. Engraved, lithographed.

20c red (engraved); black, blue, green & yellow (lithographed)

CO 138 red omitted 375.00
as above, plate block of 4 —
Scott No. 2045a
Quantity: 320-400

a) b)

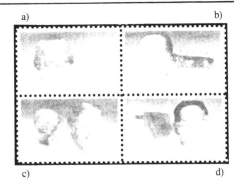

c) d)

Inventors. September 21, 1983. Se-tenant block of 4. Engraved, lithographed.

20c black (engraved); salmon (lithographed)

   a) Charles Steinmetz
   b) Edwin Armstrong
   c) Nikola Tesla
   d) Philo T. Farnsworth

CO 139 block of 4, black (engraved) omitted 600.00
as above, plate block of 4 —
as above, Zip block of 4 —
any single (a-d), black (engraved) omitted 125.00
Scott No 2058b
Quantity: 200+ blocks of 4 reported

a) b)

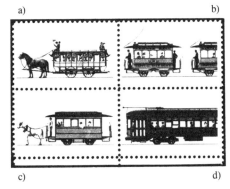

c) d)

Streetcars. October 8, 1983. Se-tenant block of 4. Engraved, lithographed.

20c black (engraved); black, magenta, yellow, blue (lithographed)

   a) First Streetcar
   b) Early Electric Streetcar
   c) Bobtail Streetcar
   d) St. Charles Streetcar

CO 140 block of 4, black (engraved) omitted 650.00
as above, any single (a-d) 100.00
Scott No. 2062b
Quantity: 120+ blocks of 4 reported

AMERIPEX. May 25, 1985. Engraved, lithographed.

22c black, blue & red (engraved); gray & beige (lithographed)

CO 141 black, blue & red (engraved)
omitted   *250.00*
Scott No. 2145a
Quantity: 700-800 reported

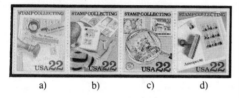

a)   b)   c)   d)

Stamp Collecting. January 23, 1986. Booklet panes of 4. Engraved, lithographed.

22c black, bright green, purple, & dark blue (engraved); yellow, light blue, beige, & red (lithographed)

a) American Philatelic Association
b) Youngster with Album
c) Magnifying Glass
d) Ameripex 86

CO 142 booklet pane of 4, black omitted   *50.00*
as above, unexploded booklet of 2
panes   *100.00*
used, on first day cover   —
Scott No. 2201b
Quantity: several thousand

a)   b)

c)   d)

Arctic Explorers. May 28, 19886. Se-tenant block of 4. Photogravure.

22c black, blue, yellow, red & gray

a)Greely
b)Kane
c)Peary, Henson
d)Stefansson

CO 143 block of 4, black omitted   —
Scott No. 2223b
Quantity: 8 blocks of 4

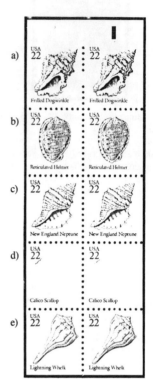

a)
b)
c)
d)
e)

Sea Shells. April 4, 1985. Se-tenant block of 4. engraved.

22c black, reddish brown & violet

a)Frilled Dogwinkle
b)Reticulated Helmet
c)New England Neptune
d)Calico Scallop
e)Lightning Whelk

CO 144 booklet pane of 10, violet omitted   —
Scott No. 2121a var
Quantity: 20-30 reported

Buying or Selling?
Consult the dealer directory at the back of the catalogue.

Presidents of the United States: I

AMERIPEX 86
International
Stamp Show
Chicago, Illinois
May 22-June 1, 1986

Presidents of the United States: III

AMERIPEX 86
International
Stamp Show
Chicago, Illinois
May 22-June 1, 1986

Presidents. May 22, 1986. Souvenir sheet of 9. engraved, lithographed.

22cdark blue (engraved); red, beige & black (lithographed)

    a)George Washington
    b)John Adams
    c)Thomas Jefferson
    d)James Madison
    e)James Monroe
    f)John Quincy Adams
    g)Andrew Jackson
    h)Martin Van Buren
    i)William H. Harrison

CO 145   sheet of 9, dark blue omitted   —
          Scott No. 2216 var
          Quantity: 2 reported

CO 146   sheet of 9, black marginal inscription omitted   —
          Scott No. 2216 var
          Quantity: 5 reported

Presidents. May 22, 1986. Souvenir sheet of 9. engraved, lithographed.

22c dark brown (engraved); red, beige & black (lithographed)

    a)Rutherford B. Hayes
    b)James Garfield
    c)Chester A. Arthur
    d)Grover Cleveland
    e)Benjamin Harrison
    f)William McKinley
    g)Theodore Roosevelt
    h)William H. Taft
    i)Woodrow Wilson

CO 147   sheet of 9, black marginal inscription omitted   —
          Scott No. 2218 var
          Quantity: n/a

Where possible, illustrations of actual error stamps were used. They are bordered in black. Where photos of errors were unavailable, illustrations of normal stamps were used. They appear without any border.

Navajo Art. September 4, 1986. Se-tenant block of 4. engraved, lithographed.

22c black (engraved); yellow, blue, magenta & black lithographed

a) *Navajo Blanket*
b) *Navajo Blanket*
c) *Navajo Blanket*
d) *Navajo Blanket*

CO 148 block of 4, black (engraved) omitted   *350.00*
any single (a-d), black omitted   —
Scott No. 2238b
Quantity: 150-200 blocks of 4

Pan American Games. January 29, 1987. Photogravure.

22c yellow, blue, magenta, black & metallic silver

CO 149 metallic silver omitted   —
Scott No. 2247 var
Quantity: n/a

Enrico Caruso. February 27, 1987. Photogravure.

22c black, yellow, magenta & gray

CO 150 black omitted   —
Scott No. 2250 var
Quantity: 10 reported

AIR MAIL STAMPS

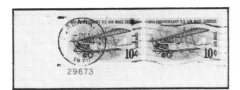

50th Anniversary of Airmail. May 15, 1968. engraved, lithographed.

10c black (engraved); blue & red (lithographed)

COA 1   red omitted   —
as above, used pair on piece LRS
(82)   6,050.00
Scott No. C74a
Quantity: very rare

☛ Caution. Dangerous fakes exist. Certificate of authenticity is essential.

First Man on the Moon. September 9, 1969. engraved, lithographed.

10c black, red, & dark blue (engraved); red, blue, light blue, gray & yellow (lithographed)

COA 2   red (litho) omitted   300.00
Scott No. C76a
Quantity: 250-300

☛ Caution. Many copies exist with red shoulder patch omitted but with litho dots of red present in the visor and yellow area of the lunar lander. All traces of red must be absent in order for the stamp to qualify as the error. Careful inspection under magnification is necessary.

National Parks Centennial. May 3, 1972. engraved, lithographed.

11c black (engraved); yellow, orange, green & blue (lithographed)

COA 3   green & blue omitted   1,850.00
as above, used   —
Scott No. C84a
Quantity: 42 reported

Progress in Electronics. July 10, 1973. engraved, lithographed.

11c black & deep red (engraved); red, brown, olive green, black & light violet (lithographed)

COA 4   red & olive green (litho) omitted   1,750.00
Scott No. C86a
Quantity: 100

Where possible, illustrations of actual error stamps were used. They are bordered in black. Where photos of errors were unavailable, illustrations of normal stamps were used. They appear without any border.

a)

b)

Wright Brothers. September 23, 1978. Vertical se-tenant pairs. engraved, lithographed.

31c black & blue (engraved); black, yellow, magenta, blue, & brown (lithographed)

a) Wrights & Biplane
b) Wrights, Biplane & Hanger

COA 5   pair, black & blue (engraved) omitted   *1,750.00*
Scott No. C92b
Quantity: 150 pairs reported

COA 6   pair, black (engraved) omitted   —
Scott No. C92c
Quantity: n/a

COA 7   pair, black, yellow, magenta, blue & brown (litho) omitted   —
Scott No. C91-2 var
Quantity: 15 pairs

a)

b)

Octave Chanute. March 29, 1979. Vertical se-tenant pairs. engraved, lithographed.

21c black & blue (engraved); black, yellow, magenta, blue, brown & (lithographed)

a) Large Portrait
b) Small Portrait

COA 8   pair, black & blue (engraved) omitted   *3,500.00*
plate block of 4, colors omitted as above on right pair   *3,500.00*
Scott No. C94b
Quantity: 5 pairs reported

MIGRATORY BIRD HUNTING STAMPS

Fulvous Whistling Duck. July 1, 1986. engraved, lithographed.

$7.50 black (engraved); yellow, brown, gray green, pale blue & light gray

COWF 1   black (engraved) omitted   —
Scott No RW53 var
Quantity: 60

POSTAGE DUE STAMPS

Numeral of Value. June 19, 1959. engraved, typographed.

COPD 1 single stamp, black omitted   *400.00*
Scott No. see note
Quantity: several hundred

Postage due stamps of this series share a common engraved background. The denomination is added in black. When black is omitted, it is not possible to identify the denomination of the error except in the case of pairs containing one normal stamp. Sheets of postage due color omitted errors usually contain a row of 10 pairs of one normal and one color omitted. The balance of the sheet consists of varying quantities of normal stamps and color omitted stamps. Once the remaining color omitted stamps are detached from the sheet, they are impossible to identify by denomination.

COPD 2   COPD 3

Numeral of Value. June 19, 1959. engraved. Typographed.

1c red (engraved); black (typographed)

COPD 2 pair, one with black omitted, one normal   *400.00*
plate block of 4, black omitted from all   —
Scott No. J89b
Quantity: 300-400

Numeral of Value. June 19, 1959. engraved, typographed.

3c red (engraved); black (typographed)

COPD 3 pair, one with black omitted, one normal   *575.00*
Scott No. J91a
Quantity: 40-60 pairs

Numeral of Value. June 19, 1959. engraved, typographed.

5c red (engraved); black (typographed)

COPD 4 pair, one with black omitted, one normal   —
Scott No. J93a
Quantity: 10 pairs

COPD 5   COPD 6

Numeral of Value. June 19, 1959. engraved, typographed.

6c red (engraved); black (typographed)

COPD 5 pair, one with black omitted, one normal   *700.00*
Scott No. J94a
Quantity: 10 pairs

Numeral of Value. June 19, 1959. engraved, typographed.

8c red (engraved); black (typographed)

COPD 6 pair, one with black omitted, one normal   *700.00*
plate block of 10, black omitted from all   —
Scott No. J96a
Quantity: 10 pairs

Numeral of Value. June 19, 1959. engraved, typographed.

10c red (engraved); black (typographed)

COPD 7 pair, one with black omitted, one normal   —
Scott No. J97 var
Quantity: 10-25 pairs reported

STAMPED ENVELOPES

Prices are for entire envelopes or cards in unused condition. The term albino refers to an embossed impression of the stamp indicia on an otherwise unprinted envelope. Albinos are not uncommon. They occur frequently, especially on certain issues, and too numerous to list comprehensively on an individual basis.

Compass. October 13, 1975. Lithographed, embossed.

10c brown & blue (light brown paper)

COSE 1 brown omitted   *150.00*
       Scott No. U571a
       Quantity: n/a

Quilt Design. February 2, 1976. Lithographed, embossed.

13c brown & blue green (light brown paper)

COSE 2 brown omitted   —
       Scott No. U572a
       Quantity: n/a

Wheat Sheaf. March 15, 1976. Lithographed, embossed.

13c brown & green (light brown paper)

COSE 3 brown omitted   —
       Scott No. U573a
       Quantity: n/a

Tools. August 6, 1976. Lithographed, embossed.

13c brown & red (light brown paper)

COSE 4 brown omitted   —
       Scott No. U575a
       Quantity: n/a

Golf. April 7, 1977. Photogravure, embossed.

13c black, blue & yellow green

COSE 5 black omitted   —
       Scott No. U583a
       Quantity: n/a

COSE 6 black & blue omitted   —
       Scott No. U583b
       Quantity: n/a

Energy Conservation. October 20, 1977. Photogravure, embossed.

13c black, red & yellow

COSE 7 black omitted   —
       Scott No. U584 var
       Quantity: n/a

COSE 8 black & red omitted   —
       Scott No. U584 var
       Quantity: n/a

COSE 9 red & yellow omitted   —
       Scott No. U584a
       Quantity: n/a

COSE 10 yellow omitted   —
       Scott No. U584b
       Quantity: n/a

U.S.A. July 28, 1978. Photogravure, embossed.

16c blue, black "Revalued to
15c" surcharge

COSE 11 black surcharge omitted   —
Scott No. U586a
Quantity: n/a

**Auto Racing. September 2, 1978. Photogravure,
embossed.**

15c black, red & blue

COSE 12 black omitted   *150.00*
Scott No. U587a
Quantity: n/a

COSE 13 black & blue omitted   —
Scott No. U587b
Quantity: n/a

COPS 14 red omitted   —
Scott No. U587c
Quantity: n/a

COPS 15 red & blue omitted   —
Scott No. U587 var
Quantity: n/a

Exists albino.

**Olympics 1980. December 10, 1979. Photogravure,
embossed.**

15c black, red & green

COSE 16 black omitted   —
Scott No. U596b
Quantity: n/a

COSE 17 black & green omitted   —
Scott No. U596c
Quantity: n/a

COSE 18 red & green omitted   —
Scott No. U596a
Quantity: n/a

COSE 19 red omitted   *225.00*
Scott No. U596 var
Quantity: n/a

Exists albino.

Bicycle. May 16, 1980. Photogravure, embossed

15c blue & maroon

COSE 20 blue omitted   *150.00*
Scott No. U597a
Quantity: n/a

**Honeybee. October 10, 1980. Photogravure,
embossed.**

15c brown, yellow, dark olive
green

COSE 21 brown omitted   *100.00*
Scott No. U599a
Quantity: n/a

**Blinded Veteran. October 11, 1981. Photogravure,
embossed.**

18c red & blue

COSE 22 black & red omitted   —
Scott No. U600 var
Quantity:

COSE 23 black & blue omitted   —
Scott No. U600 var
Quantity: n/a

COSE 24 red omitted   —
Scott No. U600 var
Quantity: n/a

COSE 25 blue omitted   —
Scott No. U600 var
Quantity: n/a

Great Seal of the United States. June 15, 1982. Photogravure, embossed.

20c black, blue & red

COSE 26 blue omitted   *125.00*
Scott No. U602 var
Quantity: n/a

Paralyzed Veterans. August 3, 1983. Photogravure, embossed.

20c black, blue & red

COSE 27 black & red omitted   —
Scott No. U605 var
Quantity: n/a

COSE 28 black & blue omitted   —
Scott No. U605 var
Quantity: n/a

COSE 29 red omitted   —
Scott No. U605 var
Quantity: n/a

COSE 30 blue omitted   —
Scott No. U605 var
Quantity: n/a

Exists albino.

AEROGRAMMES

Prices are for complete aerogrammes unless otherwise noted.

Jet Aircraft. May 1959. Inscription on reverse in 2 lines. Typographed.

10c red & blue (blue paper)

COAG 1 red omitted   —
Scott No. UC32a
Quantity: n/a

COAG 2 blue omitted   —
Scott No. UC32b
Quantity: n/a

Jet Aircraft & Globe. June 16, 1961. Typographed.

11c orange red & dark blue

COAG 3 orange red omitted   —
Scott No. UC35a
Quantity: n/a

COAG 4 dark blue omitted   —
Scott No. UC35b
Quantity: n/a

John F. Kennedy. May 29, 1967. Typographed.

11c orange red & dark blue
(blue paper)

COAG 5 orange red omitted LRS (86)   *350.00*
Scott No. UC39a
Quantity: very rare, possibly unique

COAG 6 dark blue omitted   —
Scott No. UC39b
Quantity: n/a

Human Rights Year. December 3, 1968. Photogravure.

13c black, gray, brown & orange (blue paper)

COAG 7 black omitted —
Scott No. UC42c
Quantity: n/a

COAG 8 orange omitted —
Scott No. UC42a
Quantity: n/a

COAG 9 brown omitted —
Scott No. UC42b
Quantity: n/a

U.S.A. January 4, 1974. Photogravure.

18c red, white & blue (blue paper)

COAG 10 red omitted —
Scott No. UC48a
Quantity: n/a

U.S.A. December 29, 1980. Photogravure.

30c red, blue & brown (blue paper)

COAG 11 red omitted 100.00
Scott No. UC53a
Quantity: n/a

U.S.A. May 21, 1985. Photogravure.

36c black, blue, magenta & yellow (blue paper)

COAG 12 black omitted —
Scott No. UC59 var
Quantity: 3 reported

POSTAL CARDS

Prices listed are for entire unused cards unless otherwise noted.

☛ Caution. Many postal cards were available to the public from the Postal Service in large uncut sheets. It is possible to cut individual cards from such sheets with the stamp design appearing in virtually any position. Occasionally such intentionally miscut cards are offered to the unsuspecting as errors. They are not errors and have no philatelic value.

FIPEX. May 4, 1956. Lithographed.

2c red & violet black

COPC 1 violet black omitted 375.00
Scott No. UX44b
Quantity: n/a

World Vacationland. August 30, 1963. Lithographed.

8c red & blue

COPC 2 blue omitted —
Scott No. UX49a
Quantity: n/a

U.S. Customs. February 22, 1964. Lithographed.

4c red & blue

COPC 3 blue omitted —
Scott No. UX50a
Quantity: n/a

COPC 4 red omitted —
Scott No. UX50b
Quantity: n/a

Social Security. September 26, 1964. Lithographed.

4c red & blue

COPC 5 blue omitted   —
Scott No. UX51b
Quantity: n/a

COPC 6 red omitted   —
Scott No. UX51a
Quantity: n/a

U.S. Coast Guard. August 4, 1965. Lithographed.

4c red & blue

COPC 7 blue omitted   —
Scott No. UX52a
Quantity: n/a

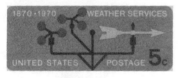

Weather Services. September 1, 1970. Lithographed.

5c black, blue, red & yellow

COPC 8 black omitted   —
Scott No. UX57c
Quantity: n/a

COPC 9 blue omitted   —
Scott No. UX57b
Quantity: n/a

COPC 9 black & yellow omitted   —
Scott No. UX57a
Quantity: n/a

America's Hospitals. September 16, 1971. Lithographed.

6c black, blue, yellow & magenta

COPC 10 blue & yellow omitted   —
Scott No. UX60a
Quantity: n/a

Philadelphia Academy of Music. June 18, 1982. Lithographed.

13c dark brown, red & cream
(buff paper)

COPC 11 dark brown & cream omitted   —
Scott No. UX96 var
Quantity: n/a

Olympics. August 5, 1984. Lithographed.

13c black, blue, yellow & magenta

COPC 12 black, yellow & magenta omitted   —
Scott No. UX100 var
Quantity: 1 reported

Rancho San Pedro. September 16, 1984. Lithographed.

13c black, blue, yellow, & magenta

COPC 13 black & blue omitted   —
Scott No. UX104 var
Quantity: n/a

AIR MAIL POSTAL CARDS

Virgin Islands. March 31, 1967. Lithographed.

6c black, yellow, blue & magenta

COAPC 1 magenta & yellow omitted —
Scott No. UXC6a
Quantity: n/a

World Jamboree. August 4, 1967. Lithographed.

6c black, yellow, blue & magenta

COAPC 2 black & blue omitted —
Scott No. UXC7b
Quantity: n/a

COAPC 3 blue omitted —
Scott No. UXC7a
Quantity: n/a

COAPC 4 magenta & yellow —
Scott No. UXC7c
Quantity: n/a

Angel Weathervane. December 17, 1975. Lithographed.

21c black, yellow, blue & red

COAPC 5 blue & red omitted —
Scott No. UXC16 var
Quantity: n/a

POSTAL CARD INVERTS

Benjamin Franklin. 1958. Lithographed, typographed.

2c red & 1c black (surcharge)

IVPC 1 black surcharge inverted —
Scott No. UX47 var
Quantity: n/a

For use by the General Electric Co. This card contains a small hole at the lower left and an advertisement printed on reverse.

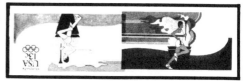

Olympics 1984. April 30, 1984. Lithographed.

13c yellow, blue, magenta & black

IVPC 2 yellow & black inverted & to the —
left of basic design
Scott No. UX102 var
Quantity: 5 reported

Extremely speculative.

INVERTED ERRORS

Columbus Landing. 1869. Engraved.

15c brown & blue

IV 1	center inverted	100,000.00
	used, center inverted	9,000.00
	Scott No. 119b	
	Quantity: rare	

Used copies usually have faults. Price above is for copy with faults. Sound specimens sell for substantially more.

NOTE: Prices for classic errors vary widely according to condition and may be substantially higher or lower than prices listed here.

IV 2	used, center double printed, one inverted LRS (86)	20,900.00
	Scott No. 119c	
	Quantity: 3 reported	

One copy is quite faulty and extensively repaired.

Declaration of Independence. April 7, 1869. Engraved.

24c green & violet

IV 3	center inverted	100,000.00
	used, center inverted	10,000.00
	Scott No. 120b	
	Quantity: very rare	

See note after IV 1.

IV 4	center inverted, imperf single LRS (86)	52,800.00
	Scott No. 120b var	

Eagle and Shield. May 15, 1869. Engraved.

30c red & blue

IV 5	center inverted	100,000.00
	used, center inverted	27,500.00
	Scott No. 121b	
	Quantity: very rare	

One hundred sets of card plate proofs of the 1869 Series (15c, 24c, 30c & 90c) exist with centers inverted. The 90c value with center inverted is known in proof form only. Market value approximately $15,000 per set of 4.

Steamship. May 1, 1901. Engraved.

1c black & green

IV 6	center inverted	10,000.00
	used, center inverted	5,000.00
	used on cover	—
	Scott No. 294a	
	Quantity:	

Train. May 1, 1901. Engraved.

2c black & red

IV 7	center inverted	35,000.00
	used, center inverted	12,500.00
	Scott No. 295a	
	Quantity: approx 150 unused; 3-5 used	

Unused copies usually have disturbed gum. Price above is for normally encountered disturbed gum.

Antique Automobile. May 1, 1901. Engraved.

4c black & brown

IV 8	center inverted **NRI**	10,000.00
	block of 4	—
	with SPECIMEN overprint	3,500.00
	Scott No. 296a	
	Quantity: 100 without overprint,	
	186 with Specimen overprint	

Distributed by the Third Assistant Postmaster General, many were marked with the word "Specimen." Additional copies were traded by the National Museum for stamps needed for their collection. Usually encountered with small faults. Price is for copy with usual small faults.

Dag Hammarskjold. October 23, 1962. Engraved.

4c black, brown & yellow

IV 9   yellow background inverted,
used on first day cover post-
marked October 23, 1962.   *1,000.00*
Scott No. 1203 var
Quantity: 10-20 reported

☛ After the discovery of the Hammarskjold error, the government re-
issued the stamp intentionally inverting the yellow. IV 9 is identical to the
re-issued stamp (Scott No. 1204 issued November 16, 1962). The only
positive way to identify the true error is by cover dated before the reis-
suance. An expert certificate is absolutely necessary for this item because
of its similarity to the special re-issue.

**Washington Crossing the Delaware. May 29, 1976.
Souvenir sheet of 5. Lithographed.**

24c multicolored

IV 10   white (USA 24c) from 4th &
5th stamps inverted   —
Scott No. 1688k
Quantity: very rare

Note. The 31c souvenir sheet of the Bicentennial issue exists with perforations inverted in relation to the design.

Candle Holder. July 2, 1979. Engraved, lithographed.

$1 dark brown (engraved);
yellow, orange & tan
(lithographed)

IV 11   candle flame inverted   —
Scott No. 1610c
Quantity: 100

AIR MAIL

Biplane. May 13, 1918. Engraved.

24c red & blue

IVA 1   center inverted   *100,000.00*
       as above, block of 4   —
       as above, center line block   —
       as above, margin block of 4
       with blue plate No.   —
       Scott No. C3a
       Quantity: 100

Prices for this stamp may vary substantially according to condition.
Each copy must be priced according to its merits. The listed price is only
an average. Select copies have sold for as much as $130,000-$145,000 during
the past year. Less desirable copies have sold for as little as $75,000.